THE SCENT OF ANGELS

WHISPERS ON THE WIND

To. Merriel

IMAGINE YOU ARE WALKING DOWN A QUIET
COUNTRY LANE ON A WARM SUMMER EVENING.
RANK WITH HIGH GRASS & WILD FLOWERS WAVE
ABOVE YOUR HEAD - STOP & LISTEN TO THE
LAZY HUM OF BEES.

NOW READ MY BOOK.

Margaret le Grange

THE SCENT OF ANGELS

WHISPERS ON THE WIND

The Life of an Irish
Horse Whisperer
as told to
MARGARET LE GRANGE

First published 2018

A CIP catalogue record for this book is available
from the British Library

ISBN 978 0 9932988 5 1

Contact Margaret by writing to
Margaret Le Grange,
Guide Light Cottage,
38 Boscaswell Village,
Pendeen, Penzance,
Cornwall TR19 7EP

Cover design by Natasha Howlette

Printed in Great Britain by Booksprint

Preface

These words were spoken to me by Colleen Flanagan, and written down word for word in the same order as originally dictated, with a few minor corrections inserted for clarification, and to make the work more readable.

Each chapter marks the end of a topic and the beginning of a new one.

This is a spirit communication received in clairvoyance messages and automatic writing: a true spirit biography. I see through the eyes of the communicator: she is showing me what she sees. I also get the sense of taste, smell, hearing and feeling, as they are experienced day by day.

The readers of this biography will travel the byways of Southern Ireland as it was in the 1800's.

Contents

1. PYKIE   9
2. FAIRY FOLK   11
3. LEPRECHAUN   13
4. WEDDINGS   16
5. HORSE FAIRS   17
6. RETURN OF KATHLEEN   22
7. TOMAS   25
8. COBH BAY   28
9. POTATO FAMINE   31
10. LIVES CHANGE   33
11. T.B.   34
12. THE WEE FOLK   36
13. NEW BEGINNINGS   40
14. THE FIRST PLANTING   43
15. RACING STABLES   48
16. ONE STEP AT A TIME   52
17. HORSE WHISPERER   53
18. MR. SINCLAIR   56
19. THE FIRST CROP   61
20. WORK BEGINS   65
21. THE STRANGER   72
22. ENGLAND   75
23. MICHAEL   82
24. RETIREMENT   88

Pykie

My name is Colleen Flanagan. I am an Irish 'Pykie', which means our family were not full Romany: my grandmother was not of the Romany tribe, and I inherited her red hair. I was born in the year 1814 in Tipperary. My Daddy was a tinker, and Mammy a half Romany who could read the palm of your hand. I grew up seeing fairies and the little green leprechaun. There were nine children. I had four brothers and four sisters; I was the last one.

We lived off the land; even as a small child I would watch my daddy set traps and snares to catch the rabbit, which was part of our daily meal. We never went hungry, as Daddy was a good provider: rabbit stew and potatoes were cooked in a large black cast iron pot hung over an open fire. Vegetables pinched from a farmer's field tasted even sweeter this way, but we never took more than we could eat in one meal: we could not run the risk of being caught red-handed.

At first there were six families on our pitch, all in brightly painted barrel-shaped wagons. There were eight ponies, many dogs, and at least twenty children of various ages, so I grew up with many playmates. We were poor, but rich in love. I was always a child who lived in my own little world: wandering off to be on my own, with my fairy friends.

Of course, the rich landowners did not look kindly on us, and we were moved on all the time, until a law was passed that gave us the right to park on common land. And so we came to be here, where I was born, on a bit of common land that ran down to a tiny spinney of slender trees at the edge of a brook that bordered the estate of a large country house on the hill.

Where we were parked was sheltered from prying eyes. At least we felt safe from the law of the landowners, for if anything went missing the tinkers were the first to be blamed; but you see we learnt well from Daddy, not to be caught.

As a tinker, Daddy also sharpened knives and ploughshares, mended pots and pans and replaced handles; he was a clever man and could turn his hand to anything. We were often paid with food: little money changed hands.

Fairy Folk

I never set foot inside a stone built house until I was twenty years old. One by one the families moved away until we were the only ones left down by the spinney. We made our living by making clothes pegs during the winter: usually my brothers did this, and us girls made baskets out of willow wisps. These were taken to market in the spring. Daddy and my brothers often went to the horse fairs, coming home with a wild pony to break in and then sell on.

I, at the age of five, began to see the wee folk. Mammy would say: 'ah, the wee folk! Remember to bless them child, when they come to you!' When I had nobody to play with, I spent many a long hour on my own, making daisy chains and playing with the little wooden doll that Mammy had made for me. It was like a peg doll: she even painted a face on it, and dressed it in rabbit skins. I loved the little doll: all of three inches high.

When the wee folk came, my doll would play with them, in the magic world I lived in. One day, I ventured further away from home. I had been told many times never to go near the water's edge in case I fell in; but running after the fairy folk I soon forgot what I had been told. So when my Mammy noticed I was missing she became frantic, fearing the worst, as the Gentry at the big house were out hunting that day. I was worried that Mammy might find me near the brook, so I rose and waved goodbye to the wee folk, and, not meaning to, I left my doll behind among the roots of the elder tree by the water's edge, where I had been sitting.

I ran, dodging the brambles, and got down on my hands and knees and crawled up the bank in the long grass. Getting to my feet, I pretended to have been asleep, and stood up, rubbing my eyes. Waving to Mammy, I answered her frantic call, running up the field, saying I was sorry, but I must have fallen asleep. Mammy was so pleased to find me, and taking her hand I skipped up the field beside her, hoping she would never find out about my lie. Only at bedtime did I notice that I did not have my doll, but could not tell Mammy the truth about it. I knew exactly where I had left the doll, and said to myself: 'ah, the fairy folk will look after her tonight, and I will get her in the morning.'

But the next day it rained, and the following day Mammy needed my help to spread the washing on the bushes to dry. And then it rained again for three more days, and by that time I had forgotten all about my doll.

Daddy and my brothers had left early in the morning to go to the horse fair in Bansha, a tiny place they often went to. They took the willow baskets and pegs we had made during the dark nights of winter. With the money from them, Daddy would buy things we needed, and some livestock: perhaps a few chickens to make a change from the rabbit stew we had every night. This time he brought back a wild horse that no one wanted, or had no time to break in.

I was six years old now. One of my sisters had left home to work as a kitchen maid at the big house. Well, Daddy came home, leading this beautiful creature. I just knew this was going to be my horse, but Daddy said: 'Colleen, you must not go near this beast as it may harm you.' But being headstrong, I had other ideas.

Leprechaun

The horse was tethered some distance from where we lived. If approached, it would lay its ears flat, and roll the whites of its eyes and show its teeth, as if warning anyone who came too close that it would get them: not to mention the damage a kick could cause. So for about a month it ate its way round the length of the chain. Daddy said: 'leave it alone, and it will calm down,' but it did not calm down: in fact I sensed it hated to be tied up, and wanted its freedom. I woke early one morning and crept outside. I walked round the area where the horse had eaten the grass, at a safe distance, and then sat down with my back to the horse, pretending not to take any notice of it: but I was very aware of its presence. I pulled up three blades of grass and started to plait them, as a distant memory came back to me, of watching Grandpappy doing this, as he won the friendship of a wild pony.

I decided that today: a fresh May day, it was time to make friends. I had an urge to do this, although I did not understand why: some things in life can't be explained: for instance, my seeing the fairies and leprechauns. As far as I knew, nobody else could see them, so perhaps I had the gift from Grandmammy, who died many years before I was born. We had all got the red hair from her and her daughter, my Mammy.

But before I go too far, let me tell you the names of my brothers and sisters, as they come into my story as well. Mary was the eldest, and then came Shamus, then Elizabeth. David and Ann were twins; then came Kathleen, Rowan and then Michael and me.

As I sat quietly, I could hear the horse coming over to me.

At first he stood a little distance behind me. I could hear his breathing, and then his chewing, but still I did not move. Then a shadow fell in front of me, and I felt a gentle nudging in my back, as if the animal was saying: 'all right: I'm here – what next?' His breath was sweet, and I felt a shiver running down my back. I was excited, thinking: fancy me, doing this! I was not afraid: if I had shown any fear he would not have come near me. I waited until his soft nose touched my cheek, and only then did I put up my hand to touch his velvet nose, still not making eye contact, just as Grandpappy had done.

Then, quietly singing a song (whose words I could not remember, so just sang 'la, la', but the song was called 'Moonlight over Galway Bay'), I half turned towards him and said: 'hello, friend,' as I slowly rose to my feet. I stood very still. He lipped my hair as if tasting me, and then lowered his head and pushed it into my chest. Slowly I moved my hand up his nose to his ears and gently rubbed them, whispering to him. He closed his eyes as if in pure happiness. Stooping a little, I gently blew I into his nostrils, making my contact with him: and so a bond was made. I called him Leprechaun.

I was so engrossed in what I was doing; I had forgotten Daddy's warnings. Lifting my arm and standing on my toes I put my hand on the horse's neck. There I found a raw patch, sticky with blood and not yet healed, and I thought: so: he has been cruelly treated. And then, talking to him, I walked away. This time I crossed the patch of grass and he followed close behind. It was not until I came to within earshot of the wagon that I saw Daddy talking wildly with his hands: he always did this; and heard the quieter voice of Mammy trying to explain that she knew I was quite safe, as I had Grandpappy's gift of horse whispering. It was then that they saw me: a small six-year-old with a head of red curls and a face full of freckles, walking with a huge horse four times taller than she was; and the horse and child seemed to be talking to one another.

When I saw them I stopped and waved. Turning, I spoke to the horse, saying I would return. But as I walked away, he continued to follow me as far as his chain would let him. In my heart I was singing, and so happy: perhaps I had the gift of horse whispering after all!

My parents did not scold me; Pappy was lost for words; but when I saw the great pride on his face and the big grin, I knew that perhaps I had done something good. That evening, they all asked what I had done to tame the horse, but I did not know. I just said: 'I did what Grandpappy did;' and Daddy said: 'but you were only three when he died: how can you remember anything?' All I knew was, it came so naturally I did not have to think about it.

The next time I went to see Leprechaun, he trotted across to meet me. I bent down and pulled a handful of sweet grass, offering it to him. He took it gently from my hand, and lowered his head for me to scratch his ears. Daddy said: 'it will soon be time to ride him, and then we will have to sell him.'

I cried out: 'you can't sell him, he is mine!'

Daddy laughed, and said there would be more ponies, and I could have the choice of one of those. I would get the chance of taming many more ponies in the years to come, but none of them were as special to me as Leprechaun was, when I was six years old.

Weddings

Sitting round the fire every evening, the family would discuss what had happened that day; and plans would be made for the next day: never once did the day start with no plan.

The years came and went, and there were two weddings to save for. One was for Elizabeth: she was a wild filly, as Daddy called her, saying she would need a man to hold her on a tight rein. The man she married was from another Romany family, and she moved away to live in Muck Ross in the county of Killarney. She was twenty-five when she wed, and my family held a Caelidh, with music and dancing.

Mary was working at the big house, and fell with child by the son of the owner. There was a lot of fuss, but Daddy would see to it that Mary was wed and well taken care of; but it would be many years before I saw her again.

Shamus at twenty-six left home and took to the road: he said he wanted to make a life for himself. I never saw him again as we were told he had gone to America and fallen in with the gold fever crowd. The next to wed was Kathleen, married to a Romany horse trader from Clonmel; but she did not settle in one place for long.

Horse Fairs

I started to go to the horse fairs with my father when I was nine years old. He did not tell anyone what I did, but I had an eye for a good horse.

Mammy took sick just before I was ten, and I stayed home to take care of her. One stormy night, Mammy died. My young life was turned upside down, and I started to find comfort in the little folk again, and disappeared for hours. Daddy got worried, as he did not know what to say or do to a young child; so he brought me a wild pony, hoping it would give me something to love. It helped a lot, and soon I was looking after the rest of the family. Ann went into service in Cork when she was eighteen years old. David stayed at home, and so did Michael.

Just before Mammy took sick, Rowan was caught stealing. He always said he could get away with anything, but this time the judge sent him to Australia for ten years. So it was only David, Michael and me left now. We were the only family on the common land now, and we moved out of view of prying eyes, further down the spinney, where there was fresher grass for the ponies.

One day, four gentlemen came by on handsome horses. They rode over the common ground, coming to a stop outside our wagon. One of them called: 'Romany, Romany, come out!' We feared the gentry, as they often caused us harm or drove us away.

I was the first to come to the door. All four and a half feet of me, I stood, hands on hips and feet apart, just daring them to come too close, spitting Romany swear words at them. They must have thought: good heavens, it's a wild cat!

The youngest of the four gentlemen got down from his horse and walked over to me. He approached slowly, smiling, and talking with words I had never heard before; then another spoke to me in English: it seemed the first man was French. With all the noise, Daddy came out, followed by David and Michael. The gentlemen had been talking in a very brash way until our men came out: perhaps they thought they would frighten me, but I stood my ground. They began speaking more quietly, asking Daddy if he could come and look at one of their horses, for word had got around that this Romany had a way with horses. The horse had fallen while out hunting, and they feared it would have to be shot. As it was a very valuable beast, the Frenchman had suggested calling upon someone who knew about horses, and that Daddy would be well paid for his trouble. 'Can you help us, please?' they asked, adding that they had heard that gypsies had magical gifts with herbs and healing.

Calling one of our dogs, we tied it to the wagon to stand guard. Daddy put a harness on the nearest pony, and I jumped up behind Daddy, holding him tight, my short arms unable to reach round his big body. All six of us galloped across the common and out onto the road that led down to the big house, going round the back into a large, well kept cobblestone stable yard. I saw for the first time that there were stone houses for the horses: one for each of them, with double doors. Later I was told they were called stables, not houses, and the posh men laughed at me for calling them houses. Daddy spoke to me in Romany, with a twinkle in his eye, saying: 'so, it took four men to get a Romany and his little child here!'

I laughed as I slid off the pony, over his tail and onto the ground. I walked over to talk to the horse; the men did not take any notice of me. Daddy went into the stable where the injured horse lay. Its front leg was badly swollen at the knee. The stable lad tried to get the horse up, but Daddy said in a sharp voice: 'no! Let it be! It should not stand until the swelling goes down! I will

go and get my herbs and rags, but I will leave my child with you.'
Calling me to stay, he mounted one of the horses and galloped
away, leaving me just standing there. I took the opportunity to
enter the dark stable where the injured horse lay.

The stable boy, who was not much older than me, once again
kicked the horse, goading it to get up. Perhaps he had never met
a gypsy child with red hair and a temper to match before: I flew
at him, swearing in Romany and spitting like a wild cat, and I
have never seen a boy run so fast, like the devil had set fire to
his tail.

All the commotion brought the men over. I stood there, hands
on hips and feet apart, and said in Romany: 'Daddy said, best
not to put any weight on his leg: let him be!' I then knelt down
and holding the horse's head between my hands, I rested my
forehead on his. In this way, I could read his thoughts. The men
tried to pull me away, but I would not move, clinging on to the
horse's bridle, so they let me be. They stood back, afraid to
tangle with such a wild cat.

I began to whisper to the horse, and he whinnied softly, pushing
his head into my tummy. He told me he was a racehorse, used
to running on the flat, not a hunter having to jump hedges. This
was how he fell, catching his foot in a hole and twisting his knee
as he came down. His owner had wanted to shoot him on the
spot, but the Frenchman had stopped him. The horse was afraid
his racing days were over, as he might never run again.

Dipping my hands in a pail of water, I shook off the drops and
gently placed my hands on the swollen knee. I felt tremendous
heat coming from the knee; and then I found myself whispering:
calling to the Little Folk as I had done when I was five years
old.

By the time Daddy came back, the swelling had gone down
quite a bit. One look from me, and Daddy understood what had
happened. That knowing look passed only between the two of us,
as he knelt down beside me. He had a handful of freshly picked

herbs, which he crushed, and spat on to make into a wodge of soft mush. This he proceeded to rub into the knee, and bind it up with rags. We stood up together. Daddy said to the men: 'it's better that you just leave him be: he will get up when the hurt has gone. I will come back tomorrow and see how he is.'

Mounting our pony, with me behind him, we rode off. I told Daddy what the stable lad had done, and begged him to bring the horse back home where I could look after him until he was better: the next day, if he could stand. Daddy said it would mean the gentlemen would be coming every day, as they might not trust us.

So began a new way for us; as our fame grew, more horses were brought to Daddy, but most of the healing was down to me. Daddy was paid well enough, and the money came in handy.

The years came and went, with me looking after the family, and going to the horse fairs with Father. David was eighteen now, and Michael had heard about the life of boxing. His bare knuckle fighting at fairs won him fame, and soon he left Ireland and went to England. It would be another thirty years before I saw him again, but not on Irish soil: more about that later.

I was sixteen, and Father had always kept my red hair cut short. I still looked lean and lanky like a boy, and went everywhere Father went; still horse-whispering, training and healing the sick horses, rubbing shoulders with the rough farmers at the fairs. No-one took me for a girl, but for boy who had a keen eye for a good horse.

When at the end of the second year David left home, news reached us that he had married, and gone to Derry for work. I had no idea where that was, and I would never see him again. It was a cruel world.

Over the years, the gentry would bring their horses to us and leave them with us. They had come to trust us, although at first they would call by every day to make sure we had not sold their horse. Mind you, we had to keep a sharp eye on the horses because of less trustworthy gypsies, in spite of the code: 'honour among thieves.' But if the horse disappeared, Daddy would have been hanged: many a gypsy ended his life at the end of a rope for stealing; we did not have the law on our side. But I am glad to say our lives continued normally.

As our name spread, we had plenty of work. Little did the gentry know, but nearly all the healing and mending was down to me. The first horse we ever tended to, came back to stay with us. It took many a long month until before we thought he was well enough to return to racing. The gentry came every day to watch his progress, and were well pleased with how he was regaining his strength. I will always remember that first horse, and, of course, Leprechaun. Although I tamed many more horses I will never forget the first one. I had become wiser, and better at the horse whispering: 'a real chip off the old block', Father would call me.

Return of Kathleen

Early one morning before the sun was up, the dogs were barking. Still half asleep, I heard voices, and to my amazement there was another Romany wagon on the common, and Kathleen was standing there with a babe in her arms and a little one hanging onto her skirts. Kathleen was the last sister to leave, at the age of seventeen. We had a 'jumping over the broomstick' ceremony for her and her man, and a fantastic feast, with everyone getting drunk: we gypsies enjoyed our Ceilidhs – any excuse for a celebration. I wept when she left.

Now she had returned – a young widow of only nineteen: her man had been killed in a brawl with another gypsy, over the price of a horse at the horse fair. Now she had nowhere to go, so she came home. It was lovely to see her, but she looked so tired, and I could see she had wept a lot. Running across the wet grass I flung my arms around her, hugging tightly, promising I would take care of her and her family. I had always hoped she would come home one day – but not like this. One of her children was a little girl, aged eighteen months, and the babe in her arms was a boy of three months.

I saw a great change in her over the next few months. When she first came, she was lost, and would not talk, but gradually the colour came back into her cheeks, and laughter filled her soul. I had my favourite sister back; the children grew; and the little girl Shannon followed me everywhere like a shadow. In my heart I often dreamed that one day I would meet a man I could love, and have children of my own. But living with Daddy and my brothers for so long, I did not have the chance of being a girl, as Daddy cut my red curls short to make me look like a boy. I often thought it was his way of holding onto me, so I never met any boys.

As the years passed, Daddy was granted permission to hunt and fish in the grounds of the big house, and we also got a small piece of land: a corner of a field, where Daddy grew potatoes. We were coming up in the world: no longer having to poach for our food. Before we got the land, we were allowed to help with the potato picking: allowed to take home only the little potatoes and only what we could carry in our hands. We managed to get quite a few, as Daddy's hands were larger than mine.

Kathleen stayed with us for nearly three years, until one day, when we got back from the horse fair, there were three more wagons parked on the common, with horses tethered out to graze, and children running about, greeting Daddy and me. At first Daddy swore, saying, 'why can't they leave us in peace,' until he recognised them as Kathleen's family. News had reached them that their son was dead, and they came searching for his wife and children. They had come to take her back, with the promise of finding Kathleen another husband. So very reluctantly Kathleen went with them, as she knew she would never meet anyone in the circles Father and I moved in: and the proof was, that I could not find a man, and I was nearly twenty!

Father had become ill, and was no longer able to do the work he once did, so I was doing a grown man's job, as well as looking after father, and travelling further afield to do my horse whispering and healing. All the time Father needed me to look after him I was tied to home. But I had an urge to move on. No longer a child but a grown woman, I grew my hair long again, and men started to notice me at long last. Life was passing me by: at my age I should be settled down with babies of my own.

One day, Daddy never got up from his bed again, and he was getting thinner every day. I tried tempting him with nice broths, but he did not want to eat. He often talked of Mammy, and was in dreadful pain, saying it felt like a wild beast eating him away inside. We were too poor to afford good medicine to take away the pain, and I could only use any herbs that I could find. And then one day Daddy joined Mammy. The wagon felt so empty without him, and I felt it was time to move on. Loading up the wagon, I collected the dogs, and the three puppies with their mother, and put them inside the wagon for safekeeping, only letting the large dog run beside me. I hitched up the cob mare, tying the other horse on the back. Greasing the wheels for a smooth run, I left early one morning, driving south.

On one of my trips, I found a quiet spot well off the road. First, I went in search of our friends. I put Daddy under the wagon, as I wanted our kin to give him a good send-off, and I did not have the money. Two days travelling brought me to my kinfolk. They gave me comfort, and a place to rest, until the send-off ceremony was arranged. Word was sent to Kathleen, Mary and Ann, but we could not find the rest of the family. My uncles made a grand send-off: Daddy would have been pleased if he was there. There was a big family gathering, and a lot of catching up to do, but I did not want to linger long. There was this place I had once seen, down Cobh Bay way. It was the most beautiful green country I had ever seen, and I had the feeling I was being called there.

While with the family, I got news that David had married a Dublin lass, and had gone to Derry. Father would have loved to know about this, but it was not to be. David had carried on like Father, sharpening knives and mending pots and pans. I caught up with all this news as passers-by came and went.

It was a late autumn day that brought Tomas O' Reilly to my side. As he was riding, his horse picked up a stone in her foot, and she went lame. He got off his horse and was walking her home when he saw me. Waving, he came over to ask if I had any water for his horse.

Tomas

Tomas was a big man, with a head of curly black hair. He was not of Romany blood, but of farming stock. The O' Reilly clan was big. Tomas had the greenest eyes I had ever seen, and I knew the moment I saw him, that I would marry this man. We warmed to each other almost instantly. Laughing together, he would touch me as he passed, and the feeling of his casual touch made me tingle with an excitement I had never felt before. What I loved most was that smile: it was bewitching… but I could not just stand here – I had work to do!

I explained to Tomas what I did, and he said: 'do what must be done, my girl – I can't go any further with her like this!'

I approached his mare the way I did with all horses, whispering softly so as not to scare the beast. By this time I stood at her head, and said: 'leave go of her reins now: she'll not move.' Calling her name, 'Shannie,' I walked round her, with my hands smoothing her sides. I felt the horse relax, and reaching her hind leg I ran my hand down it until I reached her fetlock. Whispering all the time, lifting her hoof, I ran my fingers round the soft part until I found the sharp piece of rusty metal stuck in deep. I was able to get it out, but then it bled. Calling Tomas over, I said: 'hold her like this: I must get my herbs to ease the flow of blood.'

Coming back, I placed my hand on Tomas' shoulder as I stood close to him. I left him holding the hoof, while I crushed the herbs and spat on them to make a poultice, which I pressed into the hoof, binding it with a clean rag to hold it fast. Tomas gently lowered the horse's foot, and leaving the mare to graze, I took my man back to the wagon. I had a kettle singing over the fire, and I bade him sit and drink with me, as Shannie would not travel for a while.

So, sitting opposite each other, we talked. I found myself telling him my life story, and of the little people. He did not laugh at me, but leaned forward as if not to lose a single word. At last, when I had run out of things to say, Tomas spoke. He told me he had a small farm some miles from here. His main crop was potatoes, but he had a few chickens, a goat, and his dogs.

Talking of dogs: the big male dog I had to guard me wandered over, looked at me, and laid down at Tomas' feet, as if he approved of the stranger I had welcomed to share my fire. I had never seen him do this since I had him from a puppy: he usually never left my side. At that moment the bitch came back carrying a large rabbit, which she laid at my feet: the dogs always found me rabbits for my meals.

It turned very wet and the evenings began to get chilly. I had no immediate plans as to how long I would stay in this spot; but with the darker nights, and this being my first winter on my own, I had been thinking of joining up with some more Romanies for company, for there is safety in numbers, and I was a young woman on her own.

As the evening closed in around us, I glanced at the horse. She was still not putting her full weight on her foot, so I suggested Tomas should bed down here, under the wagon: this pleased him greatly. After our food, which I prepared as we talked, it grew dark. I led my horses down to the stream to drink. Tomas came with me and filled a pail for his horse, and carried the pail back. I had not been used to such kindness from a man for a long time: while I was looking after Daddy, I did a man's work. I tied his horse and mine to the lee side of the wagon for shelter against the wind, and the oncoming rain I could smell on the wind.

Tomas was interested in how I did things, and offered to help; so I suggested he kept the fire going, as I was far too mixed up inside to be ready for sleep yet. I kept asking myself why I was feeling so excited: almost like the day I saw the little people for the first time. I just wanted to share my excitement with Mammy, but something told me to keep the feeling to myself. And now here it was again: I wanted to shout and sing, laugh and cry all at the same time.

We sat and talked about what we wanted for our future: we both wanted the same things, really. We both said it felt as if we had known each other all our lives. When neither of us could keep our eyes open any more, but just sat holding hands, we went to bed. I never gave it a thought that I was doing anything wrong: I was a grown woman, and there was nobody to say any different. So we started our lives together: it was just a natural thing to do. I had been so lonely since all the family had left, and with Daddy dying some five months ago, but now I had my man in my life.

Cobh Bay

Early next morning, Tomas and I broke camp, and quietly slipped into the dawn with the horses tethered behind. We made our way down to his small farm unseen by anyone, to save folk gossiping. I had never felt so happy since I first met Leprechaun. Although the sun was not shining this fine morning, I felt that I was bathed in a warm glow as we sat close to one another. Just the nearness of our bodies, so close together, made us both tingle with anticipation of things to come.

Shannie was not limping, and when he looked at her foot, Tomas could not believe his eyes, for there was no sign of injury. We talked in whispers, laughing and kissing all the time. He said he was in no hurry to share me with his kin. I was to move in with him, if that was my wish, and live as man and wife until we knew each other inside out. I said it would suit me well, but if trouble came, we could be properly wed; but I would not hold him to it if he changed his mind about marrying. On this understanding, we talked all the way back to the farm.

I happened to ask how come he was passing my wagon last evening, as nobody knew I was there. He replied that he had been visiting a brother, spotted the smoke, and went to see who had come to the area, as there had been some rough characters around before, and nobody wanted a repeat of that. He had been surprised to find a lass on her own So that is how we met – no magic spells: just curiosity – and love at first sight, had got us here now.

By midday we were travelling through the greenest fields I had ever seen, and I could smell that the air was different: Tomas said that would be the sea. I had never seen the sea, and did not know what to expect. The watery sun of winter was shining, and then we went down a rough lane, so that the wagon swayed from side to side, and the pans and everything inside were clanging together. And there was the stone house, nestling low beside the high hedges and ash trees. The roof looked green. 'That would be the clods of grass that make the roof,' Tomas said proudly: 'I built it with my own two hands, darlin',' he said, kissing me again.

We pulled into the yard, and I put the block of wood under the wheel to stop the wagon rolling forward, as the ground was uneven. Then, standing, I gazed about me. I had not visualised anything like this. I saw a neat yard; by the door on the wall hung a large yard broom – much larger than the ones we made of hazel twigs, and a wooden house that two large dogs were tied up to. When they saw my dogs, all hell broke loose. The barking was so loud, Tomas put his fingers into his mouth and blew a long, piercing whistle, and the dogs were quiet. We unharnessed the horses attached to the wagon leading them to a large stone trough of water, Tomas left them there side by side; then, opening a wooden half door in a hut, he put my dogs in there for a while, safe until morning, as there was so much to do: settling me in, cooking meals, feeding the chickens, goat, and Tomas' dogs. His youngest brother Shaun had been living with him, so other arrangements had to be made: he was sworn to secrecy about me, with a bribe to keep him quiet. He kept his word, though.

Life on the farm settled down to a quiet routine. Tomas and I were so in love, and it was coming up to Christmas before we knew it. That time of the year meant little to me, as we lived for the seasons, not the celebrations. I had no religious beliefs, so it felt strange, living in a strong Catholic community. I had never known about these things, but slowly I melted into that way of life. But I never went to their meetings, as I did not like crowds.

It was when Tomas' family came for their potatoes, that they first met me. Tomas was a year younger than me, but that did not matter. I was standing in the yard when Mr. O'Reilly rode up to me. I did not say anything to him: we just looked at each other. His eyes were just like my Tomas': I could see that he was family. His eyes looked at me from head to toe, coming to a stop at my large, pregnant belly. I knew what he was thinking, and my anger grew up inside me, ready to explode, but nothing was said, as at that moment Tomas came out, and putting his arms round me, said: 'Pa, meet my wife, Colleen.'

The tension broken, we all entered the house. Pa said what a great change he noticed in the house: 'a woman's touch,' he said. 'It's a year since we last saw you,' he said to Tomas; 'which we thought was strange: so, this is what you have been up to?' Pa came over and took my hand, saying, 'welcome to our family.' Asking him to stay and eat with us, I produced some game pie. There was to be a great gathering at Christmas, and we were both invited, as it was time for the family to meet their new member. I was not sure if I wanted to be introduced to the Reilly clan yet: in any case our first-born was due around that time. I had been on the farm for nearly a year now.

The first spring, we planted the field with potatoes. The crop was not that good, Tomas said, but I had never seen so many potatoes before, packed into sacks and put in a shed in the dark and dry to last the whole year through. Farm routines seemed so strange to me, as I had lived for the day. All the dogs were living in harmony now, but with so many more pups, that we decided to try and find homes for some of them, as eight dogs were too many. My hunting bitch still produced rabbits for the pot, and kept the foxes from the chickens, but being the only bitch meant she had too many puppies.

The loving got better every day, and we grew in love for each other; and then I was in the family way, and Tomas and I decided to wed the Romany way.

Potato Famine

I had two children, and another on the way. Being pregnant was the happiest time of my life; carrying a part of Tomas inside me drew us so close that we did not want any other company but our own.

Potato crops got worse every year: no one knew why. Shamus was three years old and Kathleen two, when disaster struck our little home. Both children took sick, as did many other people in our small community. The children died of cholera, and there was nothing I could do to save their lives. Panic swept through the other homes as the potato famine hit us hard. People were burning their homes to stop the cholera spreading – they even tried to burn my home, but I stood firm, and would not let my house be burnt; this made me an outcast among my neighbours.

It was at times like this that I missed Mammy the most – she would have known what to do; so one day, while on my own, I called out to her to help me, and the answer came back so fast: that I was to wash the furniture with soap, removing the upholstery, and burning it along with the bed blankets and our everyday clothes. Emptying the house completely, I tackled the walls that only a year ago I had painted with lime wash to bring more light into the house. When it was done we were left with only the bare cob stone walls and the roof. We were so sad to see our little home in this state; but it was for the best, and at least we could rebuild again when the cholera was gone. Tomas then gathered dry bracken, heather and straw from fields that had not been tilled for years, and lit fires on the floor in the two rooms, shutting off the holes for light and closing the door. We left it to smoulder for days, hoping that not too much of the roof would burn. We watched the blue smoke seep its way through the turfs on the roof.

We all moved back into the wagon, which had stood empty for years: ever since I first moved in with my man. I could not remember how Mammy had got all of us into this small space. Having lived in a house for so many years I had been spoiled for space; but we settled down and spent the next four years there. Tomas found it fun being a Romany: although we did not go travelling, he did learn how I had grown up.

My third child was born dead: I did not carry him to full term. It was another time of grieving for Tomas and me, but I felt perhaps the famine was to blame. We often went without proper food: our main diet had been potatoes, until we learnt to adapt to different ways of eating. Tomas set about burning the fields of rotting potatoes, and left them to go fallow for a few years; and then he ploughed in the ashes and spread seaweed thickly over the fields, and left them for four years, adding horse and cow manure to the seaweed. Tomas was good to the land; and in time it would recover: I knew we would plant again one year.

News filtered through about my family: sometimes two years late, so this was when I heard about Rowan being deported to the Penal Colonies of Australia for ten years, for stealing.

It was hard in the 1830's. Shamus had left for the Americas many years before, caught up in the Gold Rush fever. Mary had married the son of the big house, but she had become so high and mighty that she would not stoop so low as to see her Romany family ever again. Little David, who had married a Dublin lass, went north with his family to Derry, but in 1845 they all died of cholera. I was so heart broken, as I had never met his wife or seen any of my nephews or nieces: their lives blown out like candles. I knew Kathleen had married again, and was happy. Ann was in service in Dublin, and Michael was in England. Mary married and had three children.

After the death of my third baby, I became pregnant again, and had a healthy little girl. We called her Elizabeth, after Mammy.

Lives Changed

Our lives started to change; after we got over the shock of everything that had happened, we started going round the empty farms, gathering their livestock. We found a milking cow who was in a very bad way, but with my healing she soon got better, and the milk was good for Elizabeth, as I did not have enough milk for her. We made cheese from the goat's milk; we found chickens, a cock and a couple of geese, which made a good meal, although a bit tough. Then one day we found a very thin pony; it had been left harnessed to a small cart: the pony had got caught up in the harness and was near to death.

T.B.

Elizabeth was just two years old when I got sick, coughing. It was called T.B. I told Tomas what herbs to collect to ease my coughing. I became too weak to do anything, but Tomas and his brother Shaun were wonderful. Mrs. O'Reilly would come over. She did not approve of the way we lived in such cramped conditions. She once told her oldest son she felt I had brought shame on the family name. I overheard how angry Tomas had become, and made him tell me. I knew I must be careful, as my temper was never far away when his mother came over. She even suggested she should take our child back with her, but I would not let her come any closer to Elizabeth. How dare she try and interfere in our lives? Just because we did not live in a grand house, did not make me any different from them. I did not like her coming, but she told me to be grateful to her, and to climb down from my high horse!

Having got through the winter, with deep snow and hard frozen earth, I was looking forward to the spring. That winter of 1847 I had been very ill; at times I thought perhaps I would not see another spring; but I did. Tomas was at my side, giving me warming liquid to ease my coughing, and slowly I started to feel life coming back; then the spring burst upon us one day, the sun felt warm, the air fresh. Elizabeth was walking, and starting to say a few words: a really good reason to be alive.

Tomas had started taking his little daughter around with him, and made a small basket, slung across the pony's back for her to sit in safely. I often sat on the steps of the wagon watching as he showed her the first flowers, talking to her all the time. The knowledge of the country ways I had taught Tomas, he was passing on to his child. In the warm summer of 1848, we took Elizabeth down to the sea, so she could play in the sand. I found the clean sea air very good for my breathing, and while father and daughter played, I lay and soaked up the sun . While I was sick, my lovely red hair went white. Tomas had grey touches at his temples, but still had a lot of lovely black hair.

Shaun came and went; and now we were waiting for his return. Tomas' mother did not come very often, since she could not get her own way by bullying me. Some time later, I was with child again, and feeling very fit and happy. My cough had got better, and I was starting to feel myself again. When Tomas the younger was born, our Elizabeth was three years old. We called him Tam for short; he would not be our last child.

Time passed; but, deep down, I had that longing to go and find the wee folk again. I did not say anything, but Tomas saw that I was getting restless, and asked me: 'what ails you now? Your eyes have taken that far-away look: what do you seek, darlin'?' With more time on my hands, I longed to be a gypsy again, but knew this was not possible. I missed the travelling, and most of all the healing and horse-whispering which ran through my veins, making me feel restless: I could not explain it to Tomas. So one morning I rose early, harnessed the pony to the cart, and kissing Tam and Elizabeth, I slipped out into the dawn to find the wee folk.

That morning I discovered that I was pregnant again: about three months gone. Babies came with our passionate love-making. Tomas knew how to make me feel so alive; I longed for his touch, his kissing and loving. I would give my body to him, and he gave me his body: our happiest moments were when we lay in each other's arms.

The Wee Folk

I always looked forward to the spring after those long dark days of winter: like new grass springing up, the blood surged through my veins, and my heart beat faster and stronger. I had a purpose to fulfil, and like a child I felt excited once again.

I drove away from the sea: inland to the green fields. The place I was looking for lay some distance from the farm at Cobh Bay: a dingle and wee stream in a dark green wood: actually not far from where I had made camp all those years ago. I passed derelict farms and bare fields - the potato famine was wide spread – all the time heading west. The countryside was empty, but something pulled me on – oh, just a feeling – I can't explain it: as if by a magic force. The little pony knew where to go – although I was driving. We glided along the little narrow lanes until I found what I was looking for. The gate to the field was broken, hanging off its hinges. Crossing the field, the grass smelt sweet as it was crushed by the wheels of my pony cart.

I was here at long last – I knew it! It was early April; the fields were full of spring flowers: cowslips, daisies, harebells, buttercups and a few early bluebells peeped out among the tall grass. I heard bees and birdsong: I sat a while just listening to their song. It was something I had missed so much: the wildness of our fair green land. I heard first the field warbler with its throaty call, and then the cheeky chiff-chaff, and the whirring of a wren: the gypsy child was here again. I secretly prayed to get my life back to normal, and put the past sorrows behind me: the death of my three children, and the T.B. But I was still a young woman, and was pregnant with my sixth child.

Now I must find the wee folk again. Jumping down from the

cart, I hitched up the reins, tying them in a loose knot so that the pony could graze. I slipped away down to the dark valley below. I could see that no one had walked this way for a long time except for foxes and badgers – and there were lots of signs of rabbits. I should have brought my dog with me – she would have had a lovely time.

I found a dead tree covered with lush green moss, and sat down to wait. It was well past noon when a slight movement caught my eye. Although I sat quietly, I had been calling them, silently, in my mind; and now they started to gather round me. It was wonderful that I could still talk to the Wee Folk, although I did not see any leprechauns. Still, I was lucky to have made contact again, and told them of all our sorrows. I was granted a wish, and thought carefully before telling it. I felt truly blessed. I had no idea what hour of the day it was, as I could not see the sun; but very slowly, I rose and bade them farewell, promising to come again. One of the Wee Folk gave me a blessing with fairy dust, just like when I was a child.

Walking out of the wood, I got under a wire fence and climbed up the bank into the fields. The sun was still high. I called out to the pony, who responded with a whinny, but kept munching away. I lay down in the sweet grass, where bees were busy in the red clover. I must have drowsed off to sleep, dreaming of Mammy and Daddy, and when I was a child. I suddenly felt a warm breath on my face, and opened my eyes to see a large soft nose nuzzling my hair: the pony had come to find me. The sun had started to sink behind the hills: it was time to go home.

The journey home did not take so long; I was winding my way between high hedgerows and down narrow lanes, overgrown now because no farmers were using them. Now and then I would smell wood smoke, or hear a voice like a whisper on the wind: not catching any words, but only the sound. Then the wind changed direction and I could smell the tang of the sea, and I knew I was nearly home.

I met Tomas at the end of the little cart track. It was dark now, and my man had got worried that I had not returned before dark, and had come to meet me. He jumped up beside me, kissing me, saying: 'it was a long day without you, my darlin';' but then he looked at me and laughed. 'Why, lass, you look so young again: you must have met the Wee Folk, and they've cast their magic on you! Your eyes are laughing: I've got my lovely Colleen back again!'

'Yes, I do feel young again,' I said; 'and tonight I will tell you everything that happened today: also, I'm with child again!' We took the pony to the trough to drink, unharnessed him, and turned him out into the field. He had eaten well today: the grass in our fields was not so lush as where I had been.

As I went into the house, I saw on the table a white piece of paper, which was a strange sight indeed. Tomas relit the oil lamp, and we sat down to rabbit stew. Memories of my day tumbled out of my mouth, words falling over each other as they all tried to get out at once. I was babbling away like a child; I felt different: younger and happier than I had been for a long time. Tomas just sat and smiled. I said: 'things are going to change: our fortunes will change – I just have this feeling, that we have turned a corner!'

And in fact, the potato famine would be over soon. It had started in1845, and ended in 1849: it was now the spring of 1849, and we had moved back into the house.

Tomas said: 'do you know what happened today while you were gone? I had a visitor; a man of gentry stock came calling;' and Tomas picked up the piece of paper and gave it to me. 'See,' he said.

'You know I can't read,' I said. 'Tell me what the words say.'

'This gentleman has just bought the manor at Kinsale, some twenty miles from here, and has heard from some Romanies of your skill in horse-whispering and healing: they talked about you for a long time. Mr. Sinclair is the gentleman's name, and he wants you to go and see him next Sunday: he will send his manservant to fetch you, and bring you home again.' He had told Tomas he wanted my advice on buying horses for breeding.

I could not believe that my wish had come true so quickly; and then Tomas was very excited as he led me to the back room; and there, behind the door, was a large sack of potatoes. I immediately picked up a potato and pressed it to my nose, shutting my eyes as I tried to remember their smell. And then the words fell out of my mouth, tumbling out so fast: 'where? How? Why?'

When I had calmed down, Tomas said Mr. Sinclair had given us them as a first payment, as I would be paid for my work. Tears welled up in my eyes: me, getting paid? I could not imagine that at all!

Tomas said I would be able to get myself a pair of shoes for the winter, as up to now I had only worn clogs made of wood, with leather straps; and bare feet all summer long. I never had shoes until I wed Tomas.

Sunday came very quickly. Tomas said he would not come with me, as he had the farm and the children to look after; but I would be just fine. Just before breakfast, a pony and trap came for me. I sat beside the driver, and we talked all the way. It seemed that Mr. Sinclair was an Englishman, and had brought the potatoes with him from England. He told me the horses I had to choose would be bred for racing. Ideas flooded my mind: but I knew I could take it all in my stride.

As we travelled, I noticed the forlorn countryside; farmhouses like ours stood, burnt, the clod roofs gone, and weeds and brambles climbed everywhere, as if nature had reclaimed the earth. I had not realised that the potato famine had spread so wide. There was not a soul to be seen; it seemed we were the only ones who had not left Ireland for America or Australia. We had our own losses, too; but I had said all along that we would get through this: and we had.

The closer we got to Kinsale, the more people we saw. The fields turned green, and I remembered why this beautiful land was called the Emerald Isle.

New Beginnings

I had got through life without the learning of reading or writing; I still believed in the old values and was happy that way. But now, was my life to change? Could I manage these changing times? But some words came to mind: 'take one day at a time:' Mammy used to say this to us as children; I often felt that Mammy was near.

Our journey took us through small hamlets of little houses: all empty now; and fields full of crosses, for the churchyards were full. So, I thought sadly, this is where the village folk are today. When I first wed, this part of the south was full of families: farmers, wives and children: oh, so many children, and now not a soul to be seen. Surely not buried beside the lane? But somewhere, some of the missing would be happy, far away in America.

Before long we had turned into a well kept lane with neat hedges. We came up a long driveway to a large house standing at the end, with fenced fields around, with strong gates. The pony's hooves changed tune as he trotted over the cobbled stable yard, and pulled up to a stop. The driver came round and held out his hand to help me down. I was somewhat shy at a stranger showing me this courtesy, as usually only my Tomas did this for me. And then the lord of the manor came out, and I was introduced to Mr. Sinclair. My first thoughts were, that I could trust this man. He welcomed me, calling me 'Mrs. O'Reilly': I had never been called this by a stranger before: but then I did not often meet strangers.

I felt embarrassed by my poor worn out frock and lack of shoes; but Mr. Sinclair did not seem to notice. He was polite; as he led me round the stable yard he talked of his grand plans for breeding the fine-boned racehorses. My work would be to go to the horse fairs all over Ireland, to find the best horses: some, he told me, were brought over from France. He asked me what I thought of the idea. He would accompany me, and I would be staying at inns while we were away. I asked how long I would be away from home. He said perhaps overnight, but I would be paid handsomely for my expert advice; and even more for the horse whispering, and care of his beasts later: money was no problem.

'And what did you think of the English potatoes?' he asked.

'It was a gift from heaven, Mister, thank you,' I said. 'My Tomas will plough, and plant them soon.'

We talked some more as we walked round his estate; and finally he said: 'will you join my wife and I for a glass of wine and a bite to eat, as it's a long way back?' I accepted, and followed him round to the kitchen, where a cook was rolling out something to cover a dish: I had no idea what she was doing. This was a different world I was stepping into – there would be so much to tell Tomas when I got home!

Food was brought to us as we sat in a small parlour overlooking sweeping lawns. I asked if all this countryside belonged to him, and he laughed: not because I was simple and had asked a stupid question, but because the splendour they took for granted had made such an impression on a gypsy.

We talked about how many days they would need me to come, and where I would stay. I suggested bringing my wagon to stay in while I was working. It was agreed; but first I had to talk it over with my man, so the next time I came I must bring Tomas and the children with me.

On the journey home, my mind was a-buzzing with thoughts: but then I let my mind wander. I was a child, taming Leprechaun; and then I was down by the spinney, and seeing the green fairies, and losing my peg doll…

And then my thoughts drifted to my brother Michael: a skinny brat with a mass of red curls, and a temper to match. He was always spoiling for a fight, and he fought dirty: teeth, nails: kicking and pulling hair... often he would start the fight, and win.

The First Planting

At daybreak the next morning, Tomas was up before the sun, with my cob mare harnessed to the plough. Tomas, with the reins round his neck and hands on the plough, stood for a second and said a prayer before urging the mare forward; and for the first time in so many years, the first clod of earth was turned over. It made his heart sing with joy as he walked behind the plough, smelling the virgin soil, dark and rich and soft, that seemed to know it was planting time again. At midday, I took him a flagon of ale, and we sat on the wall and looked over our land with new eyes.

I had not had the time to talk over the events at Kinsale, and now was not the right time: it was coming up to April: time for planting our new crop of English potatoes: a new start and new beginnings. Tomas seemed to shine with joy: yes, this was going to be a good year, for both of us. He turned and put his arm round my shoulders, and pulled me to him. 'Thank you, my darlin',' he said, 'for standing beside me through all these years of sadness and sorrow: through the dark times and now out into the light. I love you so much, my darlin'.'

I rested my head on his shoulder and kissed his neck. 'I love you, too,' I whispered in his ear.

Sliding off the wall, I went into the house and brought out our sack of golden potatoes. By this time Elizabeth had joined us, and we filled our skirts with potatoes, and as a little family walked three abreast along the furrows, planting our treasured crop; Elizabeth soon picked up the way of doing it. Up and down the rows we went, and as we girls carried on planting, Tomas came behind us filling in the rows, until the whole field was done. We planted not too many, and not too close together, leaving half a sack to plant in our second field: for we had gained some extra fields when our neighbours died, and so we enlarged our farm. Tomas had removed some stone hedges to turn several fields into one, making them easier to plough.

That evening, after we had washed, and eaten our meal, and with the farm duties done, I noticed that the days were getting longer, and the long dark nights of winter were behind us. I loved the spring, when Nature cloaked her trees in shades of green, and the first swallows flew low over the fields, and made their mud nests under the eaves of the barn. God, if there was a God, was Nature.

The O'Reillys were Catholic, but I had no interest in learning about their religion. They often said it would make them proud if I would learn their way of believing; but Tomas knew, when we were wed in the old Romany way, that I would never change my way of thinking. I once heard one of the family say: 'we don't like Colleen being a heathen: you should force her to become a good Catholic;' and once Tomas' mother said: 'it hurts us that in the eyes of God, you are not married;' but Tomas only laughed and said: 'in the eyes of Romany law we are wed; and I am very happy with how our life is, Mother!' But that is why I did not like them coming round, and why so many harsh words were spoken. I said once, when I was ill, that the man I loved and had wed was all I wanted: I did not need to be wed by their God or Church: so this is how it was left.

To get back to my story, after the evening meal, we sat down to talk about Mr. Sinclair, and I told Tomas all about what had happened, and what we had talked about. At first, a deep frown came over Tomas' face, and he said: 'I never thought that the time would come when you would want to go away to work. I am concerned that it would be dangerous, while you are so heavy with child.'

I said: 'why don't you come with me, and learn for yourself what I will be doing? I'm sure Mr. Sinclair would be understanding, as he is a family man.'

Tomas replied: 'I know you have a special magical gift, and you have waited so long for the chance of using it. The final choice is yours; but remember it could be dangerous if a horse kicked you.'

'I am in no danger from any horse, my darlin',' I said, but Tomas went on: 'I am only thinking of your safety.'

Early next morning, soon after we had done the farm chores, we left Shaun in charge of the children and the farm, for one of our cows was due to calve that day. Our little two-field farm had grown in size, as we had adopted more neglected fields and starving livestock, for we could not let the animals die, and there was grass enough for all the beasts: and so we were building up a nice living. We had four horses, two cows, six goats, chickens and a cock, and the dogs; we even rescued a cat with three kittens. I made goat's cheese; and our children looked healthy and strong, for despite the potato famine, we were eating. Tomas was good with his hands, and, together with Shaun, removed the dividing walls from the fields we had claimed, and built more barns to shelter the livestock.

So at last ready to leave, the pony harnessed into the shafts of the cart, we waved goodbye and trotted down the lane and out of view of the farm. I wondered if I would get this job, and if Tomas would approve, and how many times I would be making this journey. I gave a little laugh at what I was thinking: it made me feel good. I said to Tomas: 'I can just hear what your mother would be saying if she could see me now! She would be horrified at me even thinking of leaving my family and going out to work: a woman, earning money: what a dreadful thought!'

Tomas said: 'better not let her know then – and we must tell Shaun to keep it to himself!'

I remembered the journey well – the empty homes still stood

as before: except I did smell wood smoke, and we looked to see a man in his early thirties mending the roof of a house, so it looked as if some people had come back. At least we would have a neighbour after nearly four years. We called out and waved, but then continued on our way towards Kinsale.

The journey took us about three hours, but at last we turned the pony into the long drive up to the Sinclair's big house. I felt at ease, but Tomas was nervous at first. We drove into the stable yard, where there was a group of people waiting to welcome us. The manservant came forward to help me down, and then Mr. Sinclair came, and shook hands with Tomas. They seemed to become friends straight away: there was none of this boss-and-the-worker feeling, but as if we were all just common folk. As I said, when I first met him, I knew we would work side by side as equals. The men talked and I was left on my own; so I walked round the yard with the stable lad, telling him what I did, and how I worked with horses.

A couple of hours later I was called to the house. Tomas was there, and Mrs. Sinclair asked us to come and have our midday meal with them, and so we were led through the kitchen where the cook was working, and into the parlour where I had first gone. A little girl, dressed neatly in black, with a white apron, came in with a tray of boxty bread and yellow cheeses, and a hot drink called 'tea.' This was what the English drank: it tasted a bit like wet hay – not that I had ever eaten wet hay, but it smelt like it. I did not like it, but did not say so.

Tomas and Mr. Sinclair talked about the planting of potatoes, while Mrs. Sinclair and I talked about our children. She said she noticed I was in the family way, and asked when my time of confinement was to be; I told her in six months' time. Mr. Sinclair started talking about his dream of breeding fine racehorses, and said to Tomas: 'and this is where I need your wife's expert knowledge.'

I had little to say, as the men did all the talking. Mr. Sinclair

46

said he had brought a trainer with him from England, but he had proved to be useless at his job and had to be sent away.

'The horses need a gentle touch: not to be broken in, in a cruel way.' He had heard of 'Colleen' from some Romanies at a horse fair: one of them had told him that what he needed was a horse whisperer. 'I had no idea what they were talking about,' Sinclair confessed, his ignorance causing much laughter among the Romanies; and then they explained, saying the best person for the job was Mrs. Colleen O'Reilly who was married to a farmer down Cobh way. 'This is how I found you. My manservant knew the country as his family came from these parts: name of Doonigan. Tomas said he had not come across the name, but he would ask about it the next time he saw his father, as the family home was in Waterford

Next, I overheard them discussing how long I should work, before the child was born. Tomas told me: 'it has been agreed that you can work for four months.' I was very upset that everything had been arranged between the men, and I had not been asked to say what I felt; so on the journey home I was seething with anger.

Racing Stables

I never lost my temper with my man; we never had cross words, but things had been taken out of my hands, and I was not going to accept it at all; so when Tomas said: 'what ails you, lass?' I replied: 'why did you talk about me as if I was not there? Surely it was for me to say if the plan was right for me?' Tomas put his arm round me, pulling me into him, kissing me and saying: 'I thought it best that some rules were laid down for your safety, as I love you, and will not be there to keep you safe. So it has been agreed that you will work for two months and then come home until the babe is born.' It sounded sensible, but I felt I knew what was best for me, and did not like being told what I could or could not do.

'So, when you go over there,' Tomas said, 'we will take your wagon. I will come with you and ride your mare home: and sometimes I can bring the children in the pony and cart with me, for a day out.'

It sounded reasonable, but I said: 'Mr. Sinclair said I would be working two days a week at most: but I've been thinking 'tis going to be hard on you, being away from the farm so much while you're carrying me back and forth!'

'Oh, I'll ask Shaun to share the journeys,' Tomas said.

Talking so much, I had forgotten where I was, but noticed we were still making our way out of Kinsale. Soon we would leave the noise and people behind us as we made our way into the quiet countryside, and home. It was almost dark now; we had been away too long. It was not safe to let the pony find its way without our help, so Tomas got down, and, taking the bridle, walked beside the pony, talking to him all the way home.

I spent the next two weeks cleaning out the wagon, and repainting it to brighten up the colours. This wagon had been Mammy and Daddy's home all their lives, so in their memory I must keep it going, so my children could take it on if they decided to take to the road later. Elizabeth was a good helper: she helped me clean out the wagon; and at home I taught her to cook, and make boxty bread from potatoes, when we had them. During the famine we had to make bread without them; but it was never the same: it was heavy, but filled the belly well.

Shaun kept us in touch with family news: he was a good friend, and never betrayed to his mother what we were doing, as he knew what trouble it would cause. He was like another brother to me. He was four years younger than Tomas. They were a big family, like all Catholic families then, with at least ten children, although the birth rate depended on the wealth of the family. Tomas and I were poor, but rich in love, as Romanies were.

Elizabeth was helpful, but made every task into a game, so it was a slower job. I needed her help as I could not bend too easily with my pregnant belly getting in the way; I was also suffering from backache, but I never told anyone, as I was keen to get on with my job. I decided to put the first real money towards better furniture, as the old stuff was no longer much use; so Tomas chopped it up for firewood for the winter.

All too soon, the day came for me to leave the farm. I was up at cock-crow, brushing the mare. (It was funny, but I had never given her a name: I had always called her 'My Girl.') So, after her coat was gleaming, I went in search of the old box of ribbons last used at Daddy's burial. Finding them, I shook them out and pressed each one against my leg to make it smooth: something I had learned from Mammy when I was a little girl. I plaited each ribbon into the mare's mane and tail. She looked real pretty now; and then I backed her into the shafts of the wagon, and harnessed her up, ready to leave as soon as Tomas was up.

Standing back, I felt so proud to be a gypsy again. It would be the first time I had taken to the road since coming here ten years ago. The gypsy blood raced through my veins and swelled my heart with pride. Tomas had never seen anything like this before, and I had to laugh at his face when he saw me and 'My Girl' ready to be off.

We had decided to leave early so that Tomas was not too long away from the farm; every day, he would stand and search the potato field for the first sign of green shoots. And today, there they were: three or four rows with a sheen of green, shining in the early morning sunlight.

Tomas was like a child, with new eyes. 'Why today?' he asked me; 'when I will not be here – and it was meant to be your day, darlin'.'

I said: 'never mind, darlin', it will give you something to take your mind off me being away.' The children ran out to wave goodbye, and I hugged them and kissed them, and said: 'I will be home again before you have really missed me: I will be away two days at the most!'

Tomas called out some last instructions to Shaun, saying: 'the potatoes are up!' Then he jumped up beside me, and, taking the reins, clicked at the horse, and we moved off down the lane, swaying and rolling, pans clanking, and a lantern swinging on its hook. Sitting close beside my man, I felt free: a real travelling gypsy again!

Soon, we were passing familiar scenes, but with a higher view. Perched high above the hedges, we could see further than before. Fields, hedges and trees all mingled into one tangled mess of neglect. As we neared the town, children ran out to look. Some of them had never seen a Romany wagon before: but the adults had, and shouts followed us down the road, of: 'tinker, be off! Go home! You are not wanted here!' I was used to it, but Tomas felt uneasy. 'Take no heed of them: wait until they find out I'm working for the gentry!' I laughed, as I held my head high, proud to be a proper gypsy.

We went on through the streets until we reached the lane up to Mr. Sinclair's house. Word must have reached the house, as many of the servants were waiting for us. A big cheer went up, and a lump formed in my throat: wouldn't Daddy and Mammy be proud of their little girl now?

We were shown where to put the wagon. 'My Girl' was taken out of the shafts, and I started removing her ribbons and putting them away so that Tomas could ride the mare back without getting stones thrown at him, as had happened on the way here; but I would never tell anyone about that.

One Step At A Time

I was afraid of what the future held for me as a woman in a man's world; and of being parted from Tomas: I had not spent a night away from my man in our ten years together. But I knew that this was what I wanted. Tomas said, as if reading my thoughts: 'you need not stay if you find it all too much,' but my gypsy blood was stubborn: I had said that I would do this, and that was that. Still, it did not change the fact that I was afraid of not being able to do it. And then Mammy's words came loud and clear: 'take one day at a time; step by step;' and I knew that if Mammy was with me I would be all right.

With 'My Girl' free of her ribbons, Tomas said: 'I must be going, lass.' He hugged me, and kissed me; and as he held me in his arms, he said 'I love you, my darlin'.' As we stood close together, the tears filled my eyes, but I tried not to show it. At that moment in time I did not know what lay ahead of me. And then Tomas was up on the horse, and waving to me. I could see tears in his eyes; he was sad, just like I was, but did not want to let me see it. I stood and watched him go. I felt lost, but was not going to admit it to anyone.

Just then, Mr. Sinclair came up, saying that I could take today off, as tomorrow we would be going to Dublin to the horse fair; 'but today, just find your way around, and rest; I promised your husband I would take care of you.' He said the bell would ring for meal time.

Horse Whispering

Mr. Sinclair put his hand on my arm, and said: 'thank you, Mrs. O'Reilly, for coming to help us.'

I said: 'perhaps you should call me Colleen: it sounds more friendly.' He smiled and said: 'thank you; but I will address you by your surname when I talk about you, and call you Colleen when we talk in private. My name is Richard, just between ourselves – all right?'

So started a new venture. I spent the morning visiting the stallions in the field. While I was there, the stable boy ran up to call me away, as it was not safe for me to be alone with the horses, as they were not broken in yet, and I was in danger. I could see he was very scared being here with me. He said the master had brought a trainer with him, but all he did was whip the horses, so: 'Master said he had to go!'

I said: 'go and sit on the fence – but don't run; just walk slowly, and watch me at my work: I am a horse whisperer.' But I could see he had no idea what I meant.

Once again I was in the field with Leprechaun, and I was six years old. My heart was beating fast, and music filled my ears. I was aware of every little sound, and as I walked forward the horses panicked and galloped away. But I just sat down with my back to them, pulling up three blades of grass and starting to plait them, just like Grandpappy had shown me when I was three years old. I sat and waited, not knowing that a crowd had gathered to watch, spellbound and silent.

I heard a horse slowly approaching, walking stiffly; I could tell he was afraid and ready to take flight; but still I just sat there. Little by little he came closer, curiosity getting the better of him.

At long last a shadow fell across me, and I could feel his warm, sweet breath on my back. Softly, I began to hum 'Moonlight over Galway Bay.' The horse came closer, and began to lip my hair, trying to attract my attention. I began talking to him in Romany, in gentle tones. Now lifting my arm, I stroked his big soft nose; he began to respond by nudging my back. Then slowly I got to my knees so that I was at eye level, running my hands up to his ears, all the time whispering in Romany, in a soft, gentle voice. I was aware of a bell ringing far away, but ignored it, as I did not want to break the spell.

That first horse was a grey stallion: a very large beast, much taller than Leprechaun; and at the end of three hours I had him walking with me, to the utter amazement of all those watching. I knew that the next time I went into the field he would just come over to me.

And then it was time for a meal, which the cook had kept warm for me. I said I was sorry I was late, but explained that when I work, I never know how long it will take. She said; 'lass, come when you like: 'tis lovely to have someone so gentle here, after that brute of a man who was here before you.' I took kindly to the cook: she reminded me of Mammy.

Later that day, I went back to the field, and called, and the grey trotted over to me. The other three began to follow, but then drew back. This time Richard was with me, and I warned him to stay outside the gate. I could see a big grin crease his face as the horse came forward, and I scratched the animal's ears as he pressed into me.

Richard held out his hand to touch the horse, but he laid back his ears and rolled the whites of his eyes and showed his teeth in a threatening manner: a warning to keep back. I said: 'it will take much longer for the horse to accept a man, for he remembers the last one, who hurt him, but in time I can cure him of his fear.' I added: 'I don't want anyone coming into the field: no whips or ropes, as you will not be able to catch them until I have done my whispering.'

By now I was feeling tired: perhaps it was the strangeness of the place, with so many people, that I just wanted to creep away and go to sleep. I had missed lunch when the bell had rung, but I was too tired to eat just yet; so making my excuses I walked back to my wagon. Opening up the double doors to let the sunlight in, I pulled down the roll of blankets for my bed; and then closing the bottom half of the door, I lay down to rest. I soon fell fast asleep: not before sending my love out to the little family I had left twenty miles away.

It was quite dark when I woke, and for a few minutes I did not know where I was: everything looked so strange, and there were no farm noises. Opening the door, I found a basket with boxty bread, hard yellow cheese and a stone jug full of cool sweet milk. I sat on the step in the cool of the evening and ate well, all the time looking at the stars. They were not so bright here as at home, but I counted the groups I knew; and then, rising, I folded away the bright cloth that had covered the food, and drank all the milk; I had not realised how hungry I was. I then walked across the field, hoping to return the basket to the kitchen, but the house was in darkness, except for one small window high up: it must be the servants' room, I thought to myself. As I turned the corner into the yard, a dog pulled at it chain and started barking. I spoke quietly to it, and it lay down again. I must not disturb the household, I thought; and left the basket at the back door.

Mr. Sinclair

Next day, I was up before sunrise – a normal time for me – and made ready for the early start with the Sinclairs. Richard was walking across the field towards me, calling: 'are you ready? We must leave for Dublin!' I found out that Richard's manservant was called Doonigan, and he came to say that his mistress had a pair of shoes for me, and that I was to go to the house to collect them.

Today I was to find at least three brood mares at the horse sales, but we had to get to the fair early to get the best ones. Mrs. Sinclair came out with the shoes, which fitted well, and I was glad of them today. Mrs. Sinclair climbed up beside me in the back of the carriage, and Richard sat in front with Doonigan, and off we went. The journey was very bumpy, and as we swayed from side to side, Richard apologised, but said he was in a hurry: we would take it more slowly on the way back. I felt sick. Mrs. Sinclair chatted away, all through the trip, but I only said a few words. She told me that today she had left her daughter Mel with a governess: she had to explain to me what a governess was. The journey soon passed, and I was glad to climb out onto steady ground.

My back was painful again, and the baby was kicking a lot. All I wanted to do was lie down, but that was not possible, so I put a brave face on it, and walked into the enclosure in the field. It was lovely, meeting up with so many familiar faces. Everyone wanted to know what I was doing here, and were surprised when I told them I was working for this Englishman, choosing brood mares for his breeding stables. I also caught up on some family news.

There were hundreds of people there, and I thought: if only Daddy could see me now: no longer disguised as a boy, but in my own right as a woman: yet still a Romany at heart. Forgetting the sickness I felt, I pushed my way to the front. I knew how much I was to spend on each mare, and I would choose the best.

That day I forgot the time and almost got carried away with the Romany gathering; but then Richard was at my elbow, and I was looking for good breeding mares: our target was three. I spotted a young mare; she was black as the darkest night, with two white socks and a small star on her nose: she surely was the prettiest girl I saw. I pointed her out to Mr. Sinclair, who went to find her owner, who was happy with a guinea; and so we found our first mare. The other two were a chestnut, and a grey: she was more expensive than then other two, as the Irish believe that a grey was a lucky winner: I hope they are right.

We left Doonigan in charge of the horses and went to an alehouse for some food. I was very glad to sit down. I think Mrs. Sinclair knew I was tired. It had been a long day, and I was looking forward to going home to the farm. I honestly hadn't thought this was going to be so hard. If I had not been pregnant this would have been an enjoyable day, but I found it very tiring. It was all I could do to eat the game pie, so whispered: 'can I take it home with me, as I don't want to waste good food?' I wrapped it in the folds of my frock, much to the amusement of the Sinclairs. I was worried about Tomas waiting for me to return, but Richard said: 'I told him not to come, but to wait three days, as I knew that we might not be back in time; besides, three long journeys in one day would be too much for you, in your condition.'

With three beautiful mares tied behind us, we made our way out of Dublin. I had never been there before, but Mrs. Sinclair said we had no time to look around this time. However, I was only too eager to get back to my wagon and lie down, as by now, what with all the jostle of the fair, and the standing about, all I wanted to do was get off my feet and lie down. I wondered if I would be able to last another two months: I did not want to lose another baby through not taking care of myself; and it was not long since I had been laid low with the T.B.; I still felt low and got tired too fast. Like all mothers, I had a feeling about this baby: that this one was a boy: he certainly kicked like one, which made me tired.

When we got back, I made my excuses and slipped away back to my little home for some peace, and to go to sleep, as on the bumpy journey home it was all I could do to keep my eyes open. Rolling my blankets out, I slipped off my shoes, thinking it was nice to feel the air round my toes again, and lay down to sleep.

Tomas's voice mingled with my dreams, until it became real, and I woke with a start, seeing my lovely man by my side. We were in each other's arms, kissing as we had done that October day, many years ago. 'Come, lass; time to get going: the farm is waiting for us!'

I said I must arrange a time when I should return, but Tomas said: 'it's all arranged with the boss: come now, we must make haste!'

Rolling up my blankets and putting my new shoes together, I wrapped a shawl round my shoulders, and with the help of a strong hand I was up in the seat beside my Tomas, and heading down the road which would take us home. I noticed a basket at my feet, with the same pretty cloth over the top. The question in my eyes brought the reply: 'the cook gave me this: she thought perhaps you might be too tired to cook when you got home.'

Also, in a neatly folded piece of paper, were five shiny coins: my first wage, for three days' work. I held them in my hand, turning them over and over, feeling the coldness of the metal; I had never seen anything so pretty. I took Tomas' hand and placed the coins in it. 'You take it, darlin',' I said; 'I have no pocket for its safe-keeping. I thought perhaps we could get some nice chairs and a bed with it, if that's to your liking?'

'That will be lovely: you need a good bed, and some nice things; but let us not forget other things. This money is more than I have seen in all my life; we must save some before we let it go to our heads!'

'And let's not say that we have any money, either: you know what folks are like,' I said.

I was expected to return to the Sinclairs in two weeks. Mr. Sinclair had told Tomas he wanted to put the mares in with the stallions and see if mating would take place. They would be allowed to settle before we got on with the horse whispering: there would be plenty of time for that later. Mr. Sinclair had been advised to split the horses into pairs, and put them in different fields to prevent any fighting. I had never heard of such a thing, and had to smile, saying to myself: 'horses are not like people!'

'I suppose he will buy some more brood mares later?' I asked.

'In two weeks you'll go to another country horse fair, where Sinclair has heard that some horses are being shipped over from France, and from further afield,' said Tomas; 'the stock should be worth looking at: but only after you are well rested.'

When we got home, I lifted the basket down; it was much heavier than I expected. In it were two large brown loaves and a whole game pie, a large piece of meat and some cheeses. I could nor believe my eyes; we could almost hold another Caelidh, there was so much food! We could eat like the gentry now.

Elizabeth ran out of the house and into my arms; and she was so excited to see me. I told her that next time Daddy came for me, she could come, too, so she could play with Mrs. Sinclair's little girl Mel – I had talked about this with Mrs. Sinclair on our way back from Dublin. I had also asked if I could bring Tam with me to work after my child was born, so that I could teach him the gift of horse whispering, as I had been only five years old when I started.

I had also told Mrs. Sinclair about my childhood, my brothers and sisters, and how at the age of five I had seen the Wee Folk. She had laughed and said: 'so there really are fairies? Because,' she explained, 'when we first came here, Mel was only two years old, and she kept saying she could see little people on the lawn at twilight. We agreed with her, but we never saw anything. I did not believe in fairies then: but you say you have seen them, so perhaps I am wrong!'

First Crop

'Come and see! The potatoes are all up, and growing!'

I put the basket on the table, out of reach of the dogs, who would have smelt the meat from a mile away. Closing the door behind me, I walked across the yard and over to the first field beyond the gate. Tomas was like a child, with happiness glowing in his eyes. 'Look at what's happened, darlin', since you've been away!' he said. I could see rows of green shoots, and my heart sang for joy: so many wonderful things had happened today, I could hardly take them all in. I asked how long it would take before they were ready to dig up. Tomas laughed, and said; 'we'll have to wait at least three months – about the same time the baby comes.' Every day, Tomas walked the fields, looking for any signs of the black rot; but they grew into healthy, strong plants.

I made one more trip to Kinsale to choose six more mares, but then decided I did not think I could do any more until after the baby was born. I was much larger with this pregnancy than before, and was getting more exhausted this time: I put this down to the sickness two years before.

The first crop of potatoes was ready in late summer, and I gave birth to Daniel at the same time: we called him Danny. He was a healthy, large baby, with a mass of black curls, and an armful of joy to us all. Elizabeth was now six years old, and Tam was three.

News soon spread that we had grown our first crop: Tomas went out one morning to find a small crowd of people gathering: some had baskets. I had no idea where they had all come from: I didn't think we had any neighbours: I had never seen any, except for that young man many months ago.

The day before, Tomas had been out to dig up the first potato plant, finding beautiful white-skinned fruit without a single blemish of black spots. We ate well that night. Tomas had said: 'we'd better not say we have any potatoes yet, until we are sure they are good.' I can only think someone must have been watching us, for the word to spread so fast.

The crowd was mostly poor people; but faces we did not know. We could not send them away, so Tomas said: 'all right, our crop must be dug; so if you dig a row at a time, I will let you have a few to take home in payment.' A fight flared up: some of the menfolk tried to argue and demand more, but Tomas said: 'there will be no fighting: there's plenty for all. Let us thank God for His bountiful kindness;' and everyone bowed their head in prayer. Then they all walked into the field: many had brought forks with them.

I stood with Danny in my arms, and watched as they bent forward, hands searching through the soil, with little cries of joy as the large white potatoes were taken out of the ground, and soon there was much laughter and talking. Shaun stood at one end of the field and Tomas at the other. In a few short hours, the once green field was gone. The leather buckets and baskets were full.

Then quietly, Tomas spoke, telling them that they should put aside the smaller potatoes, to set shoots for next year's planting, for once all the potatoes were eaten, there would be no more. Cider in stone jars, that seemed to appear from nowhere, were passed round; and then a woman and her man got up and danced a jig, with some folk clapping, and someone singing a tune; and there was much laughter and merrymaking.

When they had all gone their separate ways, Shaun and Tomas spread the potatoes out on the ground. It was a lovely crop: the first of many to come. We sorted out the ones we could eat, and the rest were put into heavy sacks and stored away in the barn for next year's planting. Shaun took a sack home to his parent. So ended our first season of potatoes: but it was thanks to the

Sinclairs at Kinsale, and the English potatoes, that we were back on our feet again. I put a few of the potatoes by for the Sinclairs, as a thank you.

I was looking forward to the summer of next year, when I would have more time with Danny. The time soon passed, and Danny took his first steps. I knew I wanted to return to Kinsale at some time and teach Tam the horse whispering, but not until he was five years old. Danny would be old enough to leave with Elizabeth then, and she would love to play Mammy to him.

I had not heard from the Sinclairs for three years, but somehow I was not surprised when a black horse and trap turned up at the farm one day: the Sinclairs had come over for a visit. We were in the middle of sweeping down the farmyard, and Tam was all grimed up: filthy he was; but nothing a splash of water wouldn't clean.

There had been more building onto the house to make room for our growing family, but I felt ashamed that my home was so poor, and that I had nothing to offer my guests, but they did not seem to mind. Mrs Sinclair had brought me a large bundle of her old frocks, and some that her daughter had grown out of, but they were too small for Elizabeth. I thought I would cut down one of the other frocks to fit her. These gowns were a gift: she no longer needed them, and she said she hoped I was not embarrassed. I blushed at her kindness; the dresses were so pretty. I said: 'no one has ever given me such lovely things before!' She said she thought it better to bring them to me, instead of waiting until I came over. I ran into the barn and picked up the sack of potatoes we had put by for the Sinclairs.

Mr. Sinclair was very pleased with the potatoes. By now Tomas had come into the yard, and hands were shaken in greeting. While we women folk talked, Tomas showed Mr. Sinclair round his farm. The men talked awhile, and then Mr. Sinclair came over to say that the breeding had been successful: one or two of the mares had foals, and it was time for the horse whispering to start. The horse were used to seeing people, but, as promised, no one had attempted to break them in, and it was time for me to come back, if I was still willing. And of course I was: I had only been waiting to be told when to come.

So, in the next two days, I packed up a couple of the new frocks for myself, and a few things for Tam. Tomas and I had talked about Tam coming with me, and he said it would do the lad good to learn something, rather than just running wild round the farm. He was older than I was when I started, but he did show a kindness to horses, which was a good sign.

So, early the next day, the three of us set off for Kinsale, leaving Elizabeth, Shaun and Danny behind. I felt very well in myself: it had done me good to have a long rest. I was looking forward to working again; and Tam would be able to play with Mel some of the time: they were about the same age. The journey did not seem so long now, as I had taken it many times; but it was all new to Tam. We noticed more folk had come back, as some of the houses had new clod roofs, and the garden patches looked well cared for. More voices on the wind: more neighbours would be nice.

The first day, I went up to the big house to tell the cook that I was back, and to return the basket she had so kindly given me, so full of wonderful things to eat, and told her I had brought my son with me this time, to give him the learning of my gift. We were made most welcome. Doonigan came up to say: 'welcome back!' He had become much more friendly: a real gentleman. We got talking; he said he was born in Wexford, and had met a young man named Philip O'Reilly: 'who said you had married his eldest brother, down Cobh way, and his mother wasn't too pleased you had not wed the right way: she says you're a heathen!' Paddy Doonigan started to laugh, and then added: 'the nicest heathen I've met so far!'

I smiled and said: 'let's hope that remark goes no further, please: it's hard enough for the Sinclairs to put up with the gossip of having a Romany working for them, let alone a heathen!'

Work Begins

Among the gowns Mrs. Sinclair had given me were two of the most beautiful I had ever set eyes on. Trying them on the night before I left, I twirled round in front of Tomas, dancing and stamping my feet. He sat and clapped to give me a rhythm: if only we had the fiddle I could really have shown him how I could dance: but I held the music in my heart.

The first gown was silk, so I had been told, of the darkest emerald green. It fitted me just perfectly; but it was a little short, as I was a bit taller than Mrs. Sinclair. With my hair combed out it hung down my back: no longer just red, but a lovely mixture of white and red: I had always loved my Irish hair, so thick and strong. The green gown was the same colour as my eyes, and Tomas could not take his eyes off me. Finally collapsing onto his knee, I felt so alive again, all the years of sorrow swept away.

The second gown was also of silk, and the softness of the cloth was like water running through your fingers. Its colour was dark red. It also fitted well, and had small sparkling gems around the neck: far too grand to wear around the farm, but good enough to wear to the horse fairs, I thought: people would think me quite a lady! Tomas thought they were both lovely; but I decided to take the green one with me. We laughed, and that night the lovemaking was wonderful.

So, what with all the daydreaming of what had happened the night before, I noticed we were not far from Kinsale; and with a pang in my heart I knew I would not see my man or my family for three days. Tam was getting excited, and could not wait to get down and explore. Tomas took us round to the field where the wagon was, and we opened it up to let the air in, and to air the blankets, throwing them out and over the hedge, the old Romany habits flooding back. I kissed Tomas goodbye, and went to the house to say we had arrived.

Everyone welcomed me back, all asking about the baby, and what was it, a boy or a girl? So I set about telling them all that had happened since I left them. The cook said the potatoes were just how she remembered them as a child.

At midday, Tam and I walked down the road until we came to the first field I had gone to, wondering if the grey stallion remembered me. I told Tam to sit at the edge of the field and watch, and when I felt it was safe I would call him over. He was impatient to start: he had never seen me work. I said: 'you cannot hurry this, my son: it takes time. You said you wanted to learn, so just sit and watch me closely, as I watched Granddaddy when I was three years old.'

It was high summer, and the grass was sweet and lush. I walked out to the centre of the field and sat down with my back to the horses. They were all there: mares, foals and stallions. I picked a small handful of grass, chose the three longest pieces, and started to plait them. At first nothing happened: it took quite an age before the grey stallion walked over, with easy strides. He walked right up to me; lowering his head, he sniffed my hair, and then he softly whinnied, nudging me to attract my attention. Only then did I speak to him in Romany, making contact. He moved forward until I thought he would stand on top of me. I got up and welcomed him, pressing my forehead into his nose, and whispering soft words. He was happy just to stand there. I decided to walk over to Tam, and try to make the horse accept another person: this time, a child.

As I walked across the field, the horse walked a couple of paces behind me. I had no need to hold his mane to make him follow me: he just came, like my shadow. As I reached where Tam was sitting, I made a hand sign for him to stand up. Tam just stood there not saying a word. I had told him before that he was not to make eye contact with the horse, but only look at his feet: this he did. As I stopped, I put my hand on the large beast's neck, giving him reassurance that no harm would come to him. Standing in front of Tam, I said: 'softly put your hand on his nose: use the back of your hand: this way he will know you cannot hold him.' Then I stood back while Tam spoke softly, gently rubbing the horse's nose, moving his hand up the long neck to the ears. Soon I left them and went back to the field and sat down again. The other horses had been watching, and soon ambled over to where I was sitting.

Once again I took no notice of the bell ringing for a meal. Tam was walking round the field, a small boy walking close beside the large horse. Although I could see them, I could make no contact, for fear of upsetting the other horses, who were gathering round me out of curiosity. So I began the horse whispering; the main thing was to let the horse know I meant them no harm; and there was a long way to go. This was something that could not be rushed; and I still had to teach Tam Romany. He knew a few words, but to learn the gift of the horse whisperer he must learn the correct words, and be able to sing, and I could only do this when it was quiet. I knew Tam would be good, but at the moment he was a green willow, and must be woven the correct way to do this work.

So began three years work; and the years after that flew by. Danny grew up strong: so like his father; and Tomas taught him all he knew about the farm. Elizabeth had met a young man from Kilkenny on one of our trips to market a year ago; they were courting. He was a nice, pleasant young man.

I started to do palm reading now, just like Mammy used to when we went to the fairs: these were not the horse fairs, but where we went to sell our potatoes; we also took things that we had made. I tried to teach all the Romany skills to the family, as a lot of the old crafts were dying out now. I was not needed every week at Kinsale, and had more time on my hands, so woven baskets, clothes pegs and brooms were made during the long winter evenings. Tomas started to do whittling: the old craft of carving wood, and made shillelaghs and walking sticks.

Excitement came one day, when out across the fields we saw the sails of a large cargo ship come into the bay to shelter from the storm out at sea. We got the cart out, harnessed 'My Girl', and at a right fast gallop we raced down to the bay. It was not very often we actually saw a ship come in, never being in the right place at the right time. We were not the only ones who saw the ship come in.

When Elizabeth was twenty, she married Edward O'Toole, and moved away to live in her new home at Kilkenny. It was a grand place, with lakes and castles, and trees taller than I had seen for a long time, and purple hills of heather: it was the most beautiful place for our daughter to live. Edward's family had a tanning business, so we knew Elizabeth would be well looked after. I missed her a lot at first; but then I knew that one day the children would leave home and make their way in the world. Tam was eighteen now, and a strapping lad. He had taken over from me with the horse whispering; but I was always at hand to give him the benefit of my knowledge when it came to choosing horses at the fair. He reminded me so much of my own brother Michael, with his red curls and green eyes: he was a real Pykie!

Tam spent more and more time away from home. He had settled in with the Sinclairs and lived with the stable lads. He had also met Paddy Doonigan's daughter, and wild horses couldn't drag him away. I kept in touch with Eileen and Richard Sinclair; although I called them by their first names quite freely, I would not have done so in public. They called me Colleen. Times were changing; and I found this English family very easy to get on with.

There was a long running conflict with the British invaders that came with the reign of Queen Victoria, so I was told, to tame and take control of the wild Irish folk. Many settled in the north;

fortunately not many invaded the south. I myself did not see the harm that people said they caused: I found them to be as kind as the Sinclairs.

Two years after Elizabeth and Edward married, they had a son, and called him David Edward; and then a year later another son named Tomas William, after both the granddaddies. Both children did well, and grew up to be healthy boys: so I became a Grandmammy at the age of forty-four.

Tomas fell one day and landed badly, injuring his back. We could not afford a doctor, but when Elizabeth heard, she arranged for someone to come and see him. He was told he must rest in bed for a long time; this made Tomas anxious, as he had a farm to keep running, but I told him Danny and I would keep the farm working. A year passed, and Tomas was no better, until I started to rub herbs and oil into his back; and Danny would carry his father out to sit on a seat he had made: it was like a bed, but not flat, so Tomas could see what was going on. This made so much difference to him, that he slowly got better. He would never again lift anything: but then, why should he? He had a strong son to do that. It would take three years, almost to the day, before Tomas was on his feet again; but walking with a stick.

News got to us in a letter, that Tomas read out to me, that Edward had found Michael in England. I didn't know how, but it looked as if at long last I might see my brother again.

As I could not ride any more, Tam now took over my position at the stables, breaking in the horses. The lass he was going out with was called Isobel: 'Issy' for short. I seldom saw him now, although he sometimes rode over: he was such a handsome young man. I am so proud of my children; they have done Tomas and me proud, and given so much joy.

One morning, I noticed people moving in to a little cottage down the lane that used to be the home of Annie O'Hara; I was pleased to see that Annie had come home. Her son had brought her back and mended the roof, settled her in, and then left. I walked over to see her, taking some boxty bread, a few potatoes and some wild flowers I had picked on the way. It had been ten hears since her family had come to take her away.

Walking up the path, I noticed with sadness how the neat little garden she and her husband had kept was overgrown. Knocking on the front door, I heard the shuffle of feet coming, and a small voice calling: 'who has come a-visiting?' It was a voice I knew so well: Annie had been a second Mammy to me when first I came to the farm. We greeted each other, holding tight in a warm hug. Tears ran down both our cheeks; but she composed herself, taking me by the hand and drawing me into her tiny one-roomed cottage. A small fire burnt in the grate, and a black kettle hung above.

'Come away, then, my darlin' Colleen,' she said. 'I have some thyme and honey tea on the brew – will you join me now?' She was very frail, and told me that she wanted to come home to die, where she and her husband had lived all their lives. Her son thought her mad, coming back to this tiny place, with no one to help, or care for her. He had not been able to stay too long, as he had work to get back to.

I said: 'I will take care of you – I'm only just down the lane: I'll come every day and bring you food. No; it's no trouble: I'm only too happy to have a friend I can talk to, as I live in a man's world now. I have so much to tell you – so much has happened since everyone left!'

Annie told me that they reckoned she was ninety-four. I said: 'I reckon that I'm forty-three now!' And we both laughed until the tears ran down our cheeks. It was good that she had come home again. When her husband was alive he had owned three fields and the tiny cottage, and had grown potatoes. Their land bordered on ours, with a small rough lane between. She had no one to leave it to now, and during one of our chats, she said she would like to leave it to me: her one true friend. I was thrilled, and said that for now, Danny could look after the land for her: plough the fields, and so on. This was arranged for the next spring.

One morning, after the cows had been milked, and the warm milk was in a pail, I walked across the fields by a short cut, to Annie's. I found the fire unlit, and little Annie sitting in her chair stone cold: she had joined her beloved man. As dusk fell, Danny, Tomas and I said a prayer for her soul. It was a bitter thing to say goodbye to my new-found old friend; but I knew this had been her only reason for coming home. Later, I said: 'this is all mine, now.'

Tomas and I had often spoken about when the time came for Danny to wed, and how we would move out of the farmhouse and build a small cottage a little distance from him, for the farmhouse was not big enough for two families. Often the eldest son would stay at home, not being able to find himself a wife; but I wanted all of my children to have lives of their own. I had been left at home to look after Daddy, and if he had not died, I might be there still: too old to have a family of my own.

Over the next four years, more families came back from America to Cobh Bay, as they had missed Ireland too much. Although many Irish had settled for good in America, a few came back, bringing their children. We had been growing potatoes successfully for fourteen years now, and with more fields, we were able to sell potatoes to those who wanted to start again. Over the years we had raised chickens, hatching them ourselves so we always had eggs to sell once a month at market, hence keeping a steady flow of money coming in. We were no longer poor farmers, but spent the money I had earned wisely, and saved some, putting put it away in a box under the bed. One year we had to buy a new ploughshare, as the one Tomas first had could not be mended any more. All in all I had worked for the Sinclairs for fourteen years. I enjoyed the work, but had missed the growing up of the children while I was away.

The Stranger

One day, a stranger turned up on our doorstep. Tomas was quite excited, as it was his brother, from Kerry. He was also a farmer, but with more land than Tomas. I should have known him to be family: I had not met them all as Tomas' mother had taken a disliking to me as I was a Romany, and would not take to her Roman Catholic beliefs; and she knew from the day we first met that I would not change. Tomas was not worried as he never went to his mother's church either.

Tomas introduced me to Roland, who had just heard Tomas was not able to do so much work on the farm because of his back injury. It had taken two years for the news to reach him, but now he had come over to see if he could help. I thanked him, and said that our son Danny was strong, and able to do most of the running of the farm now: in fact, we all worked.

Roland stayed a day with us. There was so much talking to do as we walked over the farm together. Tomas said he did not feel like the walk, so I took his brother around. He helped me over the stiles we had built in the walls to save opening gates. He was just like Tomas. We laughed, and I felt that this stranger could change my life. I can't explain the feeling he gave me: I just felt as if I could sing again.

As evening came, I asked him to stay. I had brought back my wagon and it was standing empty now; although I often let the Romanies stay there when they helped at harvest time. He asked if he could see inside; so, as I opened up the double doors, he stepped inside, while I remained outside. He was fascinated, just as Tomas had been all those years ago when we first met. He turned and said: 'well, Colleen Flanagan: so this is what Mother was so afraid of! Nothing to be afraid of here – this must have been a lovely home;' and bending down, he kissed me on the cheek. 'Welcome, Colleen, to my family! I only wish I had made acquaintance with you years ago!'

He was so like Tomas; and I blushed, touching my cheek where his kiss had been, and thinking, 'to be sure he has the bewitching ways, with his load of blarney! I laughed, and said: 'why not spend the night here in my wagon?'

He smiled, and said: 'thank you, my lass; that would be lovely: it will give us a chance to talk some more about what has been happening to my brother, and all my nephews and nieces.'

I knew from all the loving that Tomas had given me, and still gives me, that Roland would be the same. I would have to be careful of my heart, now, and only keep it for my man, and not be tempted by this tall dark stranger: it would not take much, I felt sure, and said to my heart: 'be careful: be aware of danger.'

My cheeks were rosy when we returned to the house; Tomas noticed straight away. 'Had a nice walk darlin'?' he asked, his eyes smiling. 'Be careful of my brother,' he added: 'he used to sweet talk all the girls when young!'

'He still does,' I said, laughing. Going over to Tomas, I kissed him full on the mouth, just as I did when lovemaking, and I felt safe once more. Tomas did not say anything, but I am sure he guessed. We never took our eyes off each other all evening, and I knew Roland could see my feelings were only for my man. I knew that tonight there would be great loving again.

Roland talked about his family: he had been a widower for three years; and had two daughters, both wed. His sister had not wed, but had come to keep house for him. He told Tomas about the rest of the family, that Tomas had not heard from in twenty years. Shaun no longer worked for us, but had gone to seek his fortune far away. We talked about our children: those who had lived and those who had died, and about my work, horse whispering. Roland was most interested in that. 'I bet Mother never knew?' he guessed.

Tomas laughed, and said: 'Shaun was sworn to secrecy never to say a word – and nor did he.'

'None of us ever knew,' said Roland; 'and Mother will not hear it from me, either!'

Retiring to the wagon, Roland went to sleep. That night as I lay in Tomas' arms, I told him what Roland had said, and how he had kissed me on the cheek. 'The blaggard!' Tomas laughed. 'I am the only one allowed to kiss my one true darlin'!'

'It meant nothing,' I said. 'I'm only telling you because we have always told each other everything: and now let it be, darlin'.'

So after a very passionate night of lovemaking, we fell asleep in each other's arms. It was so good, now that we could make love as much as we wanted without the fear of me falling with child, as I was past the age to have any more. I thought to myself, I bet Tomas' mother was not passionate like this; well-bred women did not go in for such lusty loving. I smiled as I fell asleep.

At midday Roland bade us goodbye, and said: 'I will come again;' to which Tomas replied: 'yes, to be sure: you will always be welcome, brother – as long as you remember Colleen is mine!'

England

I was looking forward to a trip that Edward and Elizabeth had arranged for me; they were going to come with me, as I did not dare go on my own. Edward's trade took him travelling a lot, so knew how to plan things properly: I would not know where to start. The date was fixed for my first journey to England. Many fears filled my mind: being on the sea, in a boat, and leaving my Ireland, and perhaps not being able to get back again; but on the other hand, there was the excitement of seeing my brother Michael again, after all this time.

Two days before I left, Tam came to visit, riding on the same stallion I had first trained and ridden. He brought a large bundle from his mistress. I was excited when I unwrapped it, to find a blue gown, and a pretty bonnet with blue ribbons. I had talked to Tomas about what I should wear for my trip, and now this had come just in time. There was a lot of talking, and catching up with the news, as it had been many years since I had worked for the Sinclairs; but we had kept in touch whenever possible, as we had become good friends, especially when Tomas was laid up with his back. They never forgot me, nor I they.

That evening, when all was quiet, and Tomas and I were sitting in front of the fire, he said: 'well, lass, are you not going to try on those grand clothes you were given today?'

I stepped out of my everyday frock, and stood naked in front of him. He rose from his chair and embraced me, slowly brushing my skin with his big powerful hands. They were rough from hard labour, but so gentle. As he kissed me, a great feeling of love flowed between us. I laughed, and said: 'time enough for that later, darlin'! I must get these clothes on and see if they fit!'

I gathered up the blue silk gown, letting it drop over my head and fall to the ground. It had a neat little waist and a lot of tiny buttons to do it up: I had to breathe in a little. Brushing out the silk, I shone like a butterfly in the firelight, as the silk seemed to come alive with different colours. I had never worn a bonnet before, and at the first try I put it on the wrong way, causing much laughter until I got it right; and tied the ribbons under my chin. I twirled and swayed in front of my lover: my man, once again. He said, quite seriously, 'you look grand, Colleen Flanagan: I hope you won't become too used to wearing such fine gowns, and want to leave me?'

I looked at him with so much love. 'Leave? What? Do you think that I would ever leave the man who brought me so much happiness and loving? Never! You aren't going to get rid of me so easy – never, my darlin'! You are all I have ever wanted!' I began to wonder if he thought the kiss his brother gave me had changed things, but snapping out of that thought, I quickly said: 'but do you like this?'

'Oh, yes, darlin': you look so pretty: I love you so much,' he said, and I replied: 'I love you more than I can ever find words to say!'

Tonight would be our last one together for about a week. I was planning to make the journey in stages: first I was going to stay the night with our Elizabeth, and the grandchildren I had never seen; and then by coach and horse to Dublin, and then by boat to Liverpool… but Edward said I would enjoy it – it would be a novelty!

At daybreak, Edward himself came for me in his fancy carriage. I was glad to see that Elizabeth had done well for herself. She was a good daughter, and never forgot her old family roots, unlike the rest of my family, who never kept in touch with each other. I had tried for so long to get in touch with my brothers and sisters, and now at long last, some twenty-five years later, I was going to meet Michael again. I often wondered what he had done with his life, and now I would meet the famous bare-knuckle fighter in Liverpool.

The journey was strange to me; but with Edward talking, the time soon passed. We stopped at an alehouse to have something to eat at midday. Edward said we were about halfway. He told me his family came from around these parts, and that he was now running the family business, his father having retired through ill health. He had one sister, who was never going to wed, as she had joined a religious order of the Sisters of Christ. I had no idea what he was talking about, so he explained: 'nuns can't marry: but we don't talk about her in the family.'(And by the way, I think you should know, he called me 'Mrs. Flanagan'.) At about early afternoon, we pulled into quite a large town with a big church, and a wide river. Except for the sea, I had never seen so much water, and it was running between the houses.

Edward and Elizabeth had such a grand house, set back off the road behind fancy gates and lovely gardens. I was envious to see such well laid out lawns, and flowers: because of the way I had lived, I only knew and admired the wild flowers, and never had a lawn of neat grass, but only fields, so all this splendour was too much for me to take in all at once. I only hope the surprise on my face did not give me away. I was very happy that Elizabeth had done so well for herself.

My grandchildren were so excited to see me: two little boys aged ten and nine. They came and took my hand, chatting non-stop, and dragged me up to their nursery, as it was called, to show me their rocking horse. I could not imagine a horse rocking in a house, and had to laugh when I was shown a big wooden horse!

The morning of our departure came, and we travelled by coach to Dunlaoghaire where the large ship lay, that would take us across the sea to England. People were climbing up a ladder like a bridge, to get on board. I was nervous: so much was new to me. I tried to hide my fear, but Elizabeth must have see the terror in my eyes, as she came to put an arm round me, assuring me that she would look after me, and that I was quite safe. The most scary part was standing so high up. Our barn roof was high, but this was even higher, and terrifying, the people on land looking like wee fairy folk. And then we were off. It was a lovely day, with blue skies and dark sea. Edward said: 'you are lucky; it will be a smooth crossing, for sometimes the sea is very rough, and everyone is sick.' The motion of the ship was rather like driving my wagon down a bumpy road, so I did not mind it so much.

Edward pointed out how far away and small the land was now; and then when I lost sight of Ireland there was nothing to see. The wind blew sticky sea spray onto my lips, and when I licked my lips I tasted the salt. Children were running along the 'decks': Elizabeth and Edward told me this word. I had learned to speak some English when I worked for the Sinclairs; but Romany was my first language, and then I had learnt to speak Gaelic, like everyone else down Cobh Bay way, so hearing English spoken again sounded strange.

Finally, after a long time, excited voices caught my attention: land had been sighted! Far away in the distance was Holyhead; an important place for the Irish, for many saints had sailed here from our land, to convert the English to Christianity. So this strange land that everyone talked about really did exist; and soon I would walk its streets; and before long I would see my brother again: I felt as excited as a child.

We had been travelling most of the day. I had no idea what time it was, and I could hardly see the sun because of so many houses and large chimneys belching out black, smelly smoke. The air smelt different now: not fresh and sweet, but choking and dirty. Edward told me that in England, people worked in deep holes under the ground, digging out black dusty stuff they called coal, which they burnt to run transport and heat their homes – give me the sweet smell of peat! I was already missing my home, but I could not say anything, as I was here to see

Michael. But I was glad that I would return to my little farm nestling in green fields, and: oh! How I missed my man!

And then I was being pushed by crowds all in a hurry to leave the ship and get onto land; at one time I got separated from Elizabeth, and started to panic, but they soon found me; and as a small family we made our way down the plank and onto the ground. I became quite afraid of the large crowds, with everyone shouting to each other: it seemed this was the way people talked to each other, in order to be heard: how could anyone live every day like this? I was grateful that Edward was in charge and knew what to do: I just followed along. He told me we would take a carriage to our lodgings in Liverpool. There were long lines of people waiting for the next stage of their transport, so Elizabeth and I went to an ale-house to get something to eat, leaving Edward to arrange everything. I would have to learn a lot of new words, to my way of thinking; and although I would not find the use of these words when I got home again, for the next few days I would be living in a new world.

Edward soon came back, and we followed him outside. The evening was drawing in fast, and by the time we reached our destination it would be quite dark. As we drove, swaying from side to side, we went down narrow streets: some were cobbled but most were mud, with large holes. At last we reached a wide river, which they told me was called the Mersey: I had to accept what I was told, as I knew no better. Here we had to wait for a ferry to take us across: another experience for me to remember. It had been a long day, full of surprises. I was beginning to think we would never get there in time, but luckily Michael's big fight was not until the following evening.

The horses panicked when they were led onto the wooden ferry, and we were all asked to step down for our own safety. It was raw and damp. Over the water hung a cold grey mist, which muffled the sound of the heavy chains pulling us from the far bank. I was told it was quite safe, but I did not feel safe, not one little bit, and was very glad to reach the far side and step onto dry land. We all climbed back onto the coach, chilled to the bone. I had never been out in the dark like this before. Different smells filled the air: the unpleasant smell of fish and cabbage, mixed with the acid smell of coal fires. It was a world I would be glad to get out of as quickly as possible: if it hadn't been for the chance of seeing Michael again, I would never have come. I wondered what Michael would think of me as well: it had been such a long time.

We turned down a muddy lane between rows of dirty house all leaning against each other. A few lighted lamps cast shadows across our path; and then my thoughts were disturbed by the coachman calling: 'The Swan and Garter!' Stepping down, steadied by Edward's hand, I shuddered and pulled my wool cape tightly round me. I was tired and cold, and all I wanted was my bed. So much had happened that I was too tired to even try and remember it now. Edward said he hoped the rooms he had booked were comfortable; but honestly, I was too tired to think much: as long as the bed was warm and soft I did not mind; but I turned to Edward and said: 'thank you for bringing me here: I'm sure everything will be perfect.'

We were shown into a back parlour with a heavy-beamed ceiling and flagstones on the floor, a heavy wooden table and rough benches. Bowls of soup were brought, with chunks of white bread. I had not tasted white bread before, and found it pleasingly good, with a much softer taste than my home-made brown bread, or boxty. Then we had cold meat – I was told it was beef – and boiled potatoes. There was far too much to eat, but at last I felt warm, and ready for my bed. We were to stay here for two nights, and return home the day after Michael's big bare-knuckle fight.

The next morning, I was woken not by the cock's crow, but by the sound of metal wheels outside, and the loud calls of people selling milk. I thought this really funny, and had to get out of bed and open the window to see what was going on. The little street was a bustle of people, and dogs were barking. The sun was not up, so the oil lamps were relit. A tap on my door brought in a young girl with a jug of hot water, and a cloth so that I could wash, so she told me. It was strange – hot water to wash with: never in my life did I have such a thing, and was not sure what to do.

A call from Elizabeth broke into my thoughts; I called her to come in. She was dressed, with her bonnet on. Sitting on the bed, we laughed at what was happening. Soon, we joined Edward, and had a small meal before going out to find the place where Michael would be that night. Edward had business to attend to during the day, so Elizabeth and I went by hansom cab, as it was called, to the museum: a large building where many strange things were kept: dead, stuffed animals from all over the world. I felt so sad to see these beautiful creatures here like this. I said to my daughter: 'what is the reason for this? What is the point?' It upset me too much, and I was glad to leave such a very sad building. I suggested perhaps we could go to one of the big gardens and sit and feed the squirrels and birds: that would bring me much more happiness.

We met up with Edward for our evening meal, and they changed clothes again. I had only brought two gowns, so I wore my dark blue one, having worn the green one, with the small bonnet to match, for travelling. We all got into a hansom cab, and set off for the fight.

Michael

It was a very tall building of many floors, and far too many rooms for me to count. There was a large room with a wooden floor covered in wood shavings, roped off into a square, which I was told was called the ring. How could it be called a ring when it had corners? It made no sense to me. People were pushing to get the best place. A rough-looking man came and said he had been sent to fetch me, at the request of Michael Flanagan, and would I come this way, please? He led me down dimly lit passageways: down and down: it felt as if we were going under the building. However, I followed quietly, my heart in my mouth.

Finally he showed me into a small, dimly lit room with a smoky oil lamp casting shadows on the walls. There sat a red-haired man. 'Michael!' I called out to him, and he spun round, his large green eyes brimming with tears of joy. He jumped to his feet, and in one swift movement he was hugging me. Both lost for words, we clung to each other. He was no longer a skinny runt, but a strong young man with a firm, muscled body: my brother. He wore his hair cut quite short; freckles covered his face, arms and hands.

'Col', he said over and over again: 'can it really be you, Col?' He always called me this when we were small, and the years fell away. 'We have so much to talk about: but time for that after my fight!' Lifting me off my feet, he kissed me, and I kissed him. He smelt strange, and I asked what he had been drinking.

'Whisky, Col: a man's drink, to put fire in his blood before the fight!'

All too soon we heard his name being shouted out from the hall, and the same man who had come to fetch me appeared again. 'Time to go, my boy!' he said. I was told to follow, to where ringside seats were ready for my family.

Of course I had seen Michael fight before, at Romany fairs, but this was different. It was ruled by a bell; and a man stood just outside the ring, to see fair play. There was no fair play: it was a dirty fight with blood spraying everywhere. Michael was the stronger of the two, and he fought hard: he had his opponent down three times, and the last time he did not get up, and there was a lot of booing and shouting. I could see that Edward was rather impressed; but Elizabeth sat with her eyes shut throughout the fight. I did not really enjoy it. We were the only two women there: this was a man's world. I did not like violence, but I had come to see my brother, so I felt I should say nothing.

The loser was carried out of the ring, and Michael's arm was raised as the winner, and it was then announced that this was Michael's last fight, and he would be returning to Ireland. He had won fourteen out of twenty fights, and was indeed a champion. Later, Michael told me that he was now forty-five, and past his prime for fighting. I was so glad to think I would now see more of him. He said he was going to Belfast on his return, to teach bare-knuckle fighting. His handsome looks had changed: he had a broken nose, and both ears were ugly and out of shape. All the fighting had changed his looks so much, and only his quiet Irish way of talking and the red curly hair and the green eyes still told me this was my brother.

We all went back to the Swan and Garter for a meat stew and apple pie, and far too much to drink. Elizabeth and I did not partake of the drink, but the men did. I noticed Michael was drinking far too much. He said it numbed the pain after a fight; but I could see more into this habit than I let on. It would be good to get him home. He surprised me by telling me he had a daughter, fifteen years of age, who lived with her mother that he had not wed. He never saw Angela now, and did not know where they were. We talked about the family: he had kept in touch with

Rowan, but lost touch with the rest of the family. Until we met again, he never knew that Daddy had died, or that I had left the Romany way and married a farmer. Michael had learned to read and write: it seemed I was the only one who could not.

The night seemed long, and soon I made my excuses and left the gathering to go to bed. Elizabeth came with me; we left the two men talking into the small hours. I knew we had to get up early to get back to the port for the boat home, and I wanted to have my wits about me this time: there were sights that I wanted to remember, to tell my children and my beloved Tomas – oh, how I missed him: his kisses and his touch that set my blood on fire!

Early next morning we were roused by knocking, and calls to say the coach driver had come and was waiting. It was a different driver this time, and the horses were quieter, and had pulled the carriage onto the ferry, and we were over it, before I knew it. I was still full of sleep, and we were all quiet – especially Edward after all his late night drinking. Jostled and bumped, we soon reached the port. The ship was at the quayside, belching out black coal smoke, which hung on the cool summer air. Bales of cotton, wood, and other goods were being loaded on board; children were racing around on deck getting under everyone's feet, their mothers not seeming to care; and soon came three long blasts on the ship's horn to say we were off.

The crossing was not so smooth this time: the ship rolled and tossed about, and people were turning a green shade and being sick over the side: soon the decks were empty. I stayed on deck, as I liked the fresh wind in my face. The children were quiet now. I stood and watched the English coast slowly disappear; and then there was nothing but huge waves, and a few brave sea birds getting blown about like autumn leaves in a gale. I was used to the wind, and gales, and being tossed about in my wagon, so I was enjoying it. I took lots of deep breaths to cleanse my lungs from the black smoke and unpleasant smells that had surrounded me in England. Halfway across, I thought the air began to smell of my home again. I saw another ship further away. It was under full sail, and racing along, blown by the wind: it was a pretty sight, to be sure. The ship's horn blew twice, and was answered by two horn blasts, as if in greeting.

And then I saw Ireland: a thin line at the edge of the sea. At first I thought it to be clouds, or my imagination; but slowly more and more land came into sight, and my heart sang for joy: for at one time, when I had seen nothing but water, I wondered if there really was any land, and if I would ever get home again.

Soon, the deck was full again, and Elizabeth and Edward were at my side. Then, taking everything in my stride, and not afraid any more, I walked down the ladder and onto dry land. The gales had gone, and clean sparkling sun shone out of a periwinkle blue sky.

And then I saw Tomas: come to take me home. The joy of being with each other was something I can't explain. I hugged and kissed my daughter, and gave Edward's cheek a kiss, which he accepted quite gracefully. I thanked him for taking me to England and looking after me so well.

Tomas had borrowed his father's carriage, leaving the pony and cart at his father's house for our return journey. It was a bit of a squeeze, and we talked of everything we did and saw, until we were at Kilkenny. We were invited to dine with them, but as it would take several more hours to get home, we said thank you, but we would rest the horses and eat, but then we must go. As we still had a long journey to take, Elizabeth suggested we stay the night with them, so her father could get to know his grandsons; and we thought this was a good idea. A lad came to take the horses to the stables for the night, and Tomas and I settled down to enjoy the company of our family.

When I first met Edward, he was a shy man, but having spent several days with him, we had warmed to one another, and he no longer called me 'Mrs. Flanagan', but 'Mama': it was good to be able to relax with him.

Early next morning, Tomas went out to harness up the horses, and found them well groomed and harnessed up ready to go. I had not noticed yesterday how lovely they were: two matching bays: but then, with Father's money he could afford the best.

At the next stop we would be meeting up with Tomas' mother. I was not fond of her, and I knew this visit was going to be hard. As I sat close to Tomas, we waved goodbye, and took the road to Wexford. Tomas said he would not let his mother upset me. It had been six years since I saw his parents, so perhaps my appearance had changed, and I might have become less fiery than in my youth: only time would tell.

Mrs. Reilly was pleased to see us, but was cool towards me, and even said: 'I see you have a very pretty dress, my dear; but the colour does not suit you.' Tomas was angry at her cruel remarks. We never told her about my horse whispering, or how I had got these gowns: that secret we hid from her. Mr. O'Reilly was kind to me; but then he always was, and he asked after the children. We ate a meal with them, left his carriage, harnessed 'My Girl' to the cart, and waving goodbye, we left for home.

It was lovely to be back in the green of my homeland, and soon we would be home again. We did not talk much, but kissed a lot. While I was away, I knew that I could never live apart from my man or leave him again, for although I had tried to enjoy all the new wonders I saw, in my heart I longed to be with my beloved man.

By mid afternoon, we were trotting down familiar lanes, waving to neighbours and friends: home again, at last! I thought it strange that nothing had changed in the six days I was gone – everything looked the same. Did I expect any change? It was only that I had missed it all so much.

All was back to normal, when a few days later, a message came from the Sinclairs, wanting me to go and help Tam with the horses, as they thought he was not up to handling the French horses that had come over by boat a week ago. Paddy came for me, and I slipped back into my old ways. I put away my fancy gowns, put on my cotton frock, and took off my shoes: I was the wild Colleen again. Tomas called me 'my Romany lass,' and we laughed. It was good to feel free again: I had to act properly while I wore the gowns, at heart no longer Colleen.

A shipment of five French horses had come: a new bloodline was being introduced to the racing stables. Tam was good, but he had let his mind wander to his new love instead of keeping it on the horses. So I set about sorting out the problem; arriving at the stable yard, I was greeted by long whinnies as the horse's heads poked out, all calling to me in their own way. I had to go to each one, kissing their soft noses, and whispering soft Romany words.

Walking down to the field, I was greeted by thundering hooves, whinnies, and a welcome that made tears come to my eyes: I had not for one moment thought they would have missed me, or even remembered me. The French horses were of a different nature to the Irish ones: they were nervous and twitchy; but three hours later they were calm: I had not forgotten my gift, even though I had not used it for a few years. I managed two horses the first day, and came back twice more to sort out the rest: and to set Tam straight, telling him he must do his job properly, for he was better at training the horses than I, although I was still the best horse whisperer in Ireland! The Sinclairs would always come first, although I sometimes went elsewhere to train horses.

Retirement

The time came when Tomas and I decided to hand the farm over to Danny. He was a young man of twenty-six now, and quite capable of running the farm. Since Tomas' back injury, he had not done a full day's work for three years; and although I had slowed down, I was still in demand for my magical herbal healing. We had a good rich green field for the sick and lame animals that were brought to me, so I did not have to go travelling again; and bit by bit the years crept up on us, both of us growing older. As a young lass, I never thought that old age would come to me. Mammy had died young: I never knew the age of my parents, but Mammy was not as old as I am, when she died.

In the wet, cold days of winter, Tomas complained a lot with his back, and was walking with two sticks now. My eyesight was failing me now: I could no longer see the flowers clearly, and I tripped over stones. 'We should both be put out to pasture now!' I told Danny one day.

Over the years since those dark days of the potato famine, Tomas and the boys reclaimed the lost, unloved ground, using the stones from hedges to build barns, and add rooms to the farmhouse to make room for the ever-growing family, and for Shaun – but he had now married and moved on. We enlarged the house that my old friend Annie O'Hara had left me, building another room onto it; and when we retired we moved out of the farmhouse and into Annie's. The farm was now Danny's home: one day he would take himself a wife from the village.

As I told you, we were the only family left in Cobh Bay when the potato famine hit us so hard; but over the years, town folk moved in and made homes for themselves. The old clod roofs were replaced by slate; windows with glass filled the empty holes in the walls; a school was built, and the village blossomed into life. The Romany wagon stood in the corner of the field: still cared for; but Danny's children played in it now: it would never take to the open road again.

Our love for each other never died, although the lovemaking ended because of Tomas' back. We still lay in one another's arms, and the kissing never died. I was seventy-five now, and I knew that my life was coming to an end. One night in mid-winter, I woke to find my Tomas quite cold beside me: he had left me in the night: he was seventy-four. His death left me utterly broken. I shut myself away and mourned him for a full year, longing to be with him. We often spent time with each other in my dreams, where we were both young again. I cried until there were no more tears: I had run dry.

I tried to give all I could to my grandchildren. Michael came down from Belfast and stayed with me for a while; and we found out that Rowan had come home from Australia. I longed to know the whereabouts of my other brothers and sisters, although many must have passed before me, as I was the youngest.

One year to the day since Tomas left me, I joined him in a bright new world, where we would be together forever.

I hope I have left my knowledge behind, for future members of my family to carry on the magic of the Romany horse whispering, and the old Romany ways of life.

1814-1890

Received from Colleen Flanagan in 2006